Introductio

Here is a wonderfully diverse an
worship material in support of
in the local church.

Wordsmiths, writers, musicians and leaders from a wide constituency
have contributed to this resource which will inspire and encourage the
people of God to worship. Yet our hope is that it might do even more
than that.

A very good pastor friend of mine once offered a comment on the
state of the Church as we head towards the millennium. Having briefly
reviewed all that has been happening over the last few decades, he
said, "As we approach the end of this century, never have we been so
over-equipped, yet so under-motivated."

The quality of our worship is wrapped up in the kind of people that we
are – our attitudes and our lifestyle. What comes from our lips must
reflect the attitude and commitment of our hearts. Indeed, real
worship can only flow from a life of service and sacrifice.

Our hope is that this collection of songs, prayer and liturgy will inspire
us all in our devotion to a sovereign God, and motivate us in renewed
determination to be strong in commitment and service.

Dave Pope

on behalf of the Spring Harvest Executive

March for Jesus — We are delighted
to include all sixteen songs written by
Graham Kendrick for March for Jesus
1997 and 1998. These songs will help the
Church to pray and proclaim the good news
of Jesus with unity and power.

Information about copyright and photocopying

Cover design by Clark and Clark, Manchester.

Layout by Spring Harvest

Printed in the UK by Halcyon, Heathfield, East Sussex

Spring Harvest wishes to acknowledge and thank the following people for their help in the compilation and production of this songbook:

Dave Pope, Robert Lamont, David Langford, Simon Moodie, Trish Morgan, David Morris, Gerry Page, Andy Piercy, Chris Redgate, Noel Richards, Laura Werts and Head Office Staff.

ISBN 1-899788-16-6
Published by Spring Harvest, 14 Horsted Square, Uckfield, East Sussex, TN22 1QL, UK.
Spring Harvest. A Registered Charity.
Distributed by ICC, Silverdale Road, Eastbourne, East Sussex, BN20 7AB, UK.

1

ABOVE THE CLASH OF CREEDS,
the many voices that call on so many names,
into these final days our God has spoken
by sending his only Son.

There is no other way
by which we must be saved;
his name is Jesus, the only saviour;
no other sinless life,
no other sacrifice,
in all creation – no other way.

Before we called he came
to earth from heaven, our maker became a man;
when no-one else could pay
　　　he bought our freedom,
exchanging his life for ours.

Beneath the cross of Christ
let earth fall silent in awe of this mystery,
then let this song arise and fill the nations:
O hear him call, 'come to me.'

Graham Kendrick
Copyright © 1995 Make Way Music

2

ALL I ONCE HELD DEAR,
　　　built my life upon,
all this world reveres and wars to own;
all I once thought gain I have counted loss –
spent and worthless now, compared to this.

Knowing you, Jesus,
knowing you, there is no greater thing:
you're my all, you're the best,
you're my joy, my righteousness;
and I love you, Lord.

Now my heart's desire is to know you more,
to be found in you and known as yours;
to possess by faith what I could not earn –
all-surpassing gift of righteousness.

Oh to know the power of your risen life,
and to know you in your sufferings;
to become like you in your death, my Lord,
so with you to live and never die!

　　　... love you, Lord.

From Philippians 3, Graham Kendrick
Copyright © 1993 Make Way Music

3

ALL THAT I AM, *I lay before you;*
all I possess, Lord, I confess,
is nothing without you.
Saviour and King,
I now enthrone you:
take my life, my living sacrifice to you.

Lord, be the strength within my weakness,
be the supply in every need
that I may prove your promises to me,
faithful and true in word and deed.

Into your hands I place the future;
the past is nailed to Calvary
that I may live in resurrection power –
no longer I but Christ in me.

James Wright
Copyright © 1994 Kingsway's Thankyou Music

4

LEADER **ALL YOU PEOPLE:**
ALL *sing unto the Lord;*
LEADER *all you nations:*
ALL *sing unto the Lord.*
Come with dancing,
come and raise your voice
to the King,
come and sing unto the Lord!

From the sun's rising to the sun's setting,
in every place, every land,
he will be glorified;
offerings of worship from every nation –
let every tribe, every tongue,
join in one song of praise.

LEADER People of Africa:
ALL sing unto the Lord!
LEADER Europe and Asia …
All of Australasia …
And all across America …
The rich and the poor will …
The weak and the strong can …
Every generation …
Every tribe and nation …

John Gibson
Copyright © 1996 Kingway's Thankyou Music

4A

The Great Commission
Matthew 28:19-20

Therefore go and make disciples of all
nations, baptising them in the name of
the Father and of the Son and of the
Holy Spirit, and teaching them to obey
everything I have commanded you.

And surely I am with you always, to the
very end of the age.

5

ALMIGHTY GOD,
to whom all hearts are open,
all desires known,
and from whom no secrets are hidden:
cleanse the thoughts of our hearts
by the inspiration of your Holy Spirit,
that we may perfectly love you
and worthily magnify;
that we may perfectly love you
and worthily magnify your holy name;
through Christ our Lord. Amen;
through Christ our Lord. Amen.

From The Alternative Service Book 1980
Copyright © 1980 The Central Board of Finance
of the Church of England

6

AMAZING GRACE – how sweet the sound
that saved a wretch like me!
I once was lost, but now am found;
was blind, but now I see.

God's grace first taught my heart to fear,
his grace my fears relieved:
how precious did that grace appear
the hour I first believed!

Through every danger, trial and snare
I have already come;
for grace has brought me safe thus far,
and grace will lead me home.

The Lord has promised good to me,
his word my hope secures;
my shield and stronghold he shall be
as long as life endures.

And when this earthly life is past,
and mortal cares shall cease,
I shall possess with Christ at last
eternal joy and peace.

John Newton
Copyright © in this version Jubilate Hymns

7

AND CAN IT BE that I should gain
an interest in the Saviour's blood?
Died he for me, who caused his pain;
for me, who him to death pursued?
Amazing love! – how can it be
that thou, my God, shouldst die for me?
Amazing love! – how can it be
that thou, my God, shouldst die for me?

'Tis mystery all! – the Immortal dies, –
who can explore his strange design?
In vain the first-born seraph tries
to sound the depths of love divine!
'Tis mercy all! — Let earth adore;
let angel minds inquire no more;
'Tis mercy all! — Let earth adore;
let angel minds inquire no more.

He left his Father's throne above –
so free, so infinite his grace –
emptied himself of all but love,
and bled for Adam's helpless race.
'Tis mercy all, immense and free;
for, O my God, it found out me;
'Tis mercy all, immense and free;
for, O my God, it found out me.

Long my imprisoned spirit lay
fast bound in sin and nature's night:
thine eye diffused a quickening ray;
I woke – the dungeon flamed with light.
My chains fell off, my heart was free;
I rose, went forth, and followed thee;
My chains fell off, my heart was free;
I rose, went forth, and followed thee.

No condemnation now I dread;
Jesus, and all in him, is mine!
Alive in him, my living head,
and clothed in righteousness divine,
bold I approach the eternal throne
and claim the crown through Christ my own;
bold I approach the eternal throne
and claim the crown through Christ my own.

Charles Wesley

8

ARE WE THE PEOPLE
who will see God's kingdom come,
when he is known in every nation?
One thing is certain,
  we are closer than before –
  keep moving on, last generation.

These are the days for harvest,
to gather in the lost;
let those who live in darkness
hear the message of the cross.

We'll go where God is sending,
we'll do what he commands;
these years that he has waited
could be coming to an end.

Noel and Tricia Richards
Copyright © 1996 Kingsway's Thankyou Music

9

AT ALL TIMES I WILL BLESS HIM,
his praise will be in my mouth –
my soul makes its boast in the Lord.
The humble man will hear of him,
the afflicted will be glad
and join with me to magnify the Lord.

  Let us exalt his name together for ever –
  I sought the Lord, he heard me
  and delivered me from my fears;
  let us exalt his name together for ever –
  O sing his praises, magnify the Lord.

The angel of the Lord encamps round
those who fear his name
to save them and deliver them from harm.

continued over…

9A

Proverbs 23:22-25

Listen to your father, who gave you
life, and do not despise your mother
when she is old.

Buy the truth and do not sell it; get
wisdom, discipline and understanding.

The father of a righteous man has
great joy; he who has a wise son
delights in him.

May your father and mother be glad;
may she who gave you birth rejoice!

Though lions roar with hunger,
we lack for no good thing:
no wonder, then, we praise him with our song.

Come, children, now and hear me
if you would see long life:
just keep your lips from wickedness and lies.
Do good and turn from evil;
seek peace instead of strife;
love righteousness and God will hear your cry.

From Psalm 34
Copyright © Stuart Dauermann

10

BE STILL,

for the presence of the Lord,
    the holy One, is here;
come bow before him now
with reverence and fear:
in him no sin is found –
we stand on holy ground.
Be still,
for the presence of the Lord,
    the holy One, is here.

Be still,
for the glory of the Lord
    is shining all around;
he burns with holy fire,
with splendour he is crowned:
how awesome is the sight –
our radiant king of light!
Be still,
for the glory of the Lord
    is shining all around.

Be still,
for the power of the Lord
    is moving in this place:
he comes to cleanse and heal,
to minister his grace –
no work too hard for him.
In faith receive from him.
Be still,
for the power of the Lord
    is moving in this place.

David J. Evans
Copyright © 1986 Kingsway's Thankyou Music

11

BEHOLD HIS LOVE.

I stand amazed and marvel at
the God of grace:
that the Alpha and Omega,
the Beginning and the End,
the Creator of the universe
on whom all life depends,
should be clothed in frail humanity
and suffer in my place.
Behold his love
and worship him,
the God of grace.

Geoff Baker
Copyright © 1996 Sovereign Music UK

12

BEHOLD THE LORD upon his throne:

his face is shining like the sun.
With eyes blazing fire, and feet glowing bronze,
his voice like mighty water roars.
    Holy, holy, Lord God, almighty:
    holy, holy! We stand in awe of you.

The first, the last, the living One,
laid down his life for all the world.
Behold, he now lives for evermore,
and holds the keys of death and hell!
    Holy, holy, Lord God, almighty:
    holy, holy! We bow before your throne.

So let our praises ever ring
to Jesus Christ our glorious King.
All heaven and earth resound as we cry,
'Worthy is the Son of God!'
    Holy, holy, Lord God, almighty:
    holy, holy! We fall down at your feet.

From Revelation 4
Noel Richards & Gerald Coates
Copyright © 1991 Kingsway's Thankyou Music

13

BLESSING AND HONOUR,

    glory and power
be unto the Ancient of Days;
from every nation, all of creation
bow before the Ancient of Days.

Every tongue in heaven and earth
shall declare your glory,
every knee shall bow at your throne in worship;
you will be exalted, O God,

and your kingdom shall not pass away,
O Ancient of Days.

Blessing and honour ...

Your kingdom shall reign over all the earth:
sing unto the Ancient of Days;
for none can compare to your matchless worth:
sing unto the Ancient of Days.

... O Ancient of Days, O Ancient of Days.

Gary Sadler and Jamie Harvill
Copyright © 1992 Integrity's Hosanna! Music/Integrity's Praise
Music/Integrity Music Europe

14

BREATHE ON ME, BREATH OF GOD:
fill me with life anew,
that as you love, so I may love
and do what you would do.

Breathe on me, breath of God,
until my heart is pure,
until my will is one with yours
to do and to endure.

Breathe on me, breath of God;
fulfil my heart's desire,
until this earthly part of me
glows with your heavenly fire.

Breathe on me, breath of God;
so shall I never die,
but live with you the perfect life
of your eternity.

Edwin Hatch
Copyright © in this version Jubilate Hymns

13A

Creation Psalm

Fill my heart as you filled the sea
Blow away the clouds that loom
    in my soul
And let the same breath
Give life to these dry bones.

Envelope me with fields
Wrap me in a mountain
Blow stars at me like kisses
Let me know your
    incomprehensible love.

Explode in my heart like a comet
Roar through me like sunlight
Break over me
    in waves of compassion
Ravish me with your passion.

Ripping the fabric of my universe
Burst my straining mind;
I cannot understand.
Love me.

14A

Ephesians 6:18

Be alert and always keep praying.

14B

Prayer of renewal

Almighty God, whose Holy Spirit
equips the Church with a rich variety
of gifts; grant that we may use them to
bear witness to Christ by lives built on
faith and love. Make us ready to live his
gospel and eager to do his will, that we
may share with all your Church in the
joys of eternal life; through Jesus
Christ our Lord.

Amen.

15

BY HIS GRACE I am redeemed,
by his blood I am made clean,
and I now can know him face to face.
By his power I have been raised:
hidden now in Christ by faith,
I will praise the glory of his grace.

Steve Fry
Copyright © 1994 Deep Fryed/Music Services/CopyCare

16

BY YOUR SIDE I would stay,
in your arms I would lay;
Jesus, lover of my soul,
nothing from you I withhold.

> Lord, I love you
> and adore you.
> What more can I say?
> You cause my love
> to grow stronger
> with every passing day.

> Lord, I love you …

Noel & Tricia Richards
Copyright © 1989 Kingsway's Thankyou Music

16A

Praise
from Psalm 72

Praise the Lord, the God of Israel:
he alone does marvellous things.

Praise his glorious name for ever;
let his glory fill the earth!

© ✝

17

CAN A NATION BE CHANGED,
can a nation be saved,
can a nation be turned back to you?

Let this nation be changed,
let this nation be saved,
let this nation be turned back to you.

We're on our knees, we're on our knees again;
we're on our knees, we're on our knees again.

We're on our knees, we're on our knees again;
we're on our knees, we're on our knees again.

Matt Redman
Copyright © 1996 Kingsway's Thankyou Music

17A

John 8: 12

Jesus said, 'I am the light of the world.
Whoever follows me will never walk in
darkness, but will have the light of life.'

18

CAN WE WALK UPON THE WATER
if our eyes are fixed on you?
There's an air of faith within us
for a time of breaking through.
Can we fly a little higher,
can we soar on eagle's wings?
Come and fan the flames of fire
that are flickering within.

Can we walk into the promise
of abundance in the land?
Take us on, beyond the river,
to the harvest you have planned;
let us see your kingdom coming
in a measure we've not seen.
There has been a time of sowing,
could this be a time to reap?

> Lead us to the promised land,
> all that's purposed, all that's planned;
> give us eyes of faith again.
> Take us onto higher ground
> and the greater things to come –
> where the eagles soar,
> and where we're finding more of you.

Can we walk into the promise …

And can we sing the songs of heaven
while we're standing on the earth:
sing within the coming kingdom,
sing and live and breathe and move?
Can we fly a little higher,
can we fly a little higher,
can we fly a little higher,
can we fly a little higher?

Matt Redman
Copyright ©1996 Kingsway's Thankyou Music

18A

Prayer For The Sick

Creator and Father of all, we pray for those who are ill.

Bless them, and those who serve their needs, that they may put their whole trust in you and be filled with your peace; through Jesus Christ our Lord.

Amen.

© Collect for the sick – ASB 1980

19

CELEBRATE, CELEBRATE, CELEBRATE,

O celebrate Jesus!

LEADER From the far corners of earth
we hear music
ALL O celebrate,
LEADER echoing over the land and sea;
ALL O celebrate,
LEADER sound of the drums awakes
a new morning,
ALL O celebrate,
LEADER calling our feet to
the rhythms of praise.
ALL O celebrate Jesus.
Celebrate, celebrate, celebrate,
O celebrate Jesus!

LEADER Out of the West come
shouts of rejoicing,
ALL O celebrate,
LEADER out of the East a loud reply;
ALL O celebrate,
LEADER over the nations a voice is calling:
ALL O celebrate,
LEADER 'worship the maker of earth and sky.'
ALL O celebrate Jesus.

LEADER We have millions of reasons to
celebrate Jesus; and I'll sing you
seven if you count from one.
Everybody count:
ALL One!

LEADER He gave up the glory of heaven,
ALL Two!
LEADER humbly became one of us,
ALL Three!
LEADER showed us the love of the Father,
ALL Four!
LEADER paid for our sins on a cross,
ALL Five!
LEADER rose from the dead victorious,
ALL Six!
LEADER ascended to heaven's throne,
ALL Seven!
LEADER poured out his spirit upon us:
ALL O celebrate Jesus.
Celebrate, celebrate, celebrate,
O celebrate Jesus – celebrate!

Graham Kendrick
Copyright © 1996 Make Way Music

20

COME AND SEE, come and see,
come and see the King of love;
see the purple robe and crown of thorns
he wears.
Soldiers mock, rulers sneer,
as he lifts the cruel cross;
lone and friendless now
he climbs towards the hill.

We worship at your feet,
where wrath and mercy meet,
and a guilty world is washed
by love's pure stream;
for us he was made sin,
oh, help me take it in;
deep wounds of love cry out,
'Father, forgive!'
I worship, I worship
the Lamb who was slain.

Come and weep, come and mourn,
for your sin that pierced him there;
so much deeper than the wounds of
thorn and nail.
All our pride, all our greed,
all our fallenness and shame –
and the Lord has laid the punishment on him.

Man of heaven, born to earth
to restore us to your heaven:
here we bow in awe beneath your searching eyes.
From your tears comes our joy,
from your death our life shall spring;
by your resurrection power we shall rise!

Graham Kendrick
Copyright © 1989 Make Way Music

21

LEADER **COME, LET US RETURN TO THE LORD;**

ALL come, let us return to the Lord;
come, let us return to the Lord,
let us return to the Lord.

As surely as the sun rises,
he will appear, he will appear;
he will come to us like winter rains
and like the spring rains that water the earth.

MEN *Come, let us return to the Lord;*
WOMEN *come, let us return to the Lord;*
ALL *come, let us return to the Lord,*
let us return to the Lord.

Though he tore us, he will heal us;
though he tore us, he will heal us:
let us return to the Lord.

LEADER *Come, let us return to the Lord ...*

Come, let us press on to know him,
walk in his ways, walk in his ways
that we may live in his presence
all of our days, all of our days.

MEN *Come, let us return to the Lord ...*

Seek him, find him, know him, love him;
seek him, find him, know him, love him:
let us return to the Lord.

Graham Kendrick
Copyright © 1996 Make Way Music

22

COME OUT OF DARKNESS
into the light;
come out of darkness into the light;
come out of darkness into the arms of love,
into the arms of love.

To a world in darkness,
to a world in pain,
at this time you've called us
your love to proclaim;
Through your willing people
to the nations say,
to the nations say:

Do not be discouraged,
see what God has done;
he is working through us,
this world shall be won.
There will be a harvest
when the nations hear –
what are they going to hear?

By the blood of Jesus
sin is washed away;
all who call upon him,
he will surely save:
this will be the promise
that the nations hear
when we sing it loud and clear.

Noel Richards and Doug Horley
Copyright © 1996 Kingsway's Thankyou Music

23

COUNTER TO THE CULTURE,
going against the flow,
finding new direction –
your kingdom is upside-down,
your kingdom is upside-down,
your kingdom is upside-down.

Justice, peace and righteousness –
the politics of your government,
where the poor are blessed
and the strong are weak,
earth is inherited by the meek.

In resistance to the spirit-of-the-age,
live a lifestyle that can be sustained;
undermine the idols
of technology and science –
the need for the latest gadget or appliance.

Women and men have equal worth:
lay down power and learn to serve!
To give is better than to receive,
cancel debts, love your enemy.

Jon Baker and Jon Birch
Copyright © 1995 Serious Music UK

24

CROWN HIM WITH MANY CROWNS,
the Lamb upon his throne,
while heaven's eternal anthem drowns
all music but its own!
Awake, my soul, and sing
of him who died to be
your saviour and your matchless king
through all eternity.

Crown him the Lord of life
triumphant from the grave,
who rose victorious from the strife
for those he came to save:
his glories now we sing
who died and reigns on high;
who died eternal life to bring
and lives that death may die.

Crown him the Lord of love,
who shows his hands and side –
those wounds yet visible above
in beauty glorified.
No angel in the sky
can fully bear that sight,
but downward bends his burning eye
at mysteries so bright.

Crown him the Lord of peace –
his kingdom is at hand;
from pole to pole let warfare cease
and Christ rule every land!
A city stands on high,
his glory it displays,
and there the nations 'Holy' cry
in joyful hymns of praise.

Crown him the Lord of years,
the potentate of time,
creator of the rolling spheres
in majesty sublime:
all hail, Redeemer, hail,
for you have died for me;
your praise shall never, never fail
through all eternity!

Matthew Bridges & Godfrey Thring
Copyright © in this version Jubilate Hymns

25

DID YOU FEEL THE MOUNTAINS TREMBLE,

did you hear the oceans roar,
when the people rose to sing
of Jesus Christ, the risen One?

Did you feel the people tremble,
did you hear the singers roar
when the lost began to sing
of Jesus Christ, the saving One?

And we can see that, God, you're moving –
a mighty river through the nations;
and young and old will turn to Jesus.
Fling wide, you heavenly gates,
prepare the way of the risen Lord!

continued over…

23A

Living God's Way

*from Exodus 20, Deuteronomy 5
and New Testament Scriptures*

'You shall have no other gods but me.'

Lord, help us to love you with all our heart, all our soul, all our mind and all our strength.

'You shall not dishonour the name of the Lord your God.'

Lord, help us to honour you with reverence and awe.

'Remember the Lord's day and keep it holy.'

Lord, help us to remember Christ risen from the dead, and to set our minds on things above, not on things on the earth.

'Honour your father and mother.'

Lord, help us to live as your servants, giving respect to all, and love to our brothers and sisters in Christ.

'You shall not commit adultery.'

Lord, help us to be honest in all we do, and to care for those in need.

'You shall not be a false witness.'

Lord, help us always to speak the truth.

'You shall not covet anything which belongs to your neighbour.'

Lord, help us to remember Jesus said, 'It is more blessed to give than to receive', and help us to love our neighbour as ourselves for his sake. Amen.

© Michael Perry ✝

Open up the doors and let the music play,
let the streets resound with singing –
songs that bring your hope,
songs that bring your joy,
dancers who dance upon injustice.

Do you feel the darkness tremble
when all the saints join in one song
and all the streams flow as one river
to wash away our brokenness?

And here we see that, God, you're moving –
a time of jubilee is coming,
when young and old return to Jesus.
Fling wide, you heavenly gates,
prepare the way of the risen Lord!

26

DON'T LET MY LOVE GROW COLD,
I'm calling out,
'light the fire again.'
Don't let my vision die,
I'm calling out,
'light the fire again.'

You know my heart, my deeds,
I'm calling out,
'light the fire again.'
I need your discipline,
I'm calling out,
'light the fire again.'

I am here to buy gold,
refined in the fire;
naked and poor,
wretched and blind, I come.
Clothe me in white,
so I won't be ashamed:
'Lord, light the fire again!'

Don't let my love ...

27

DOWN THE MOUNTAIN the river flows,
and it brings refreshing wherever it goes;
through the valleys and over the fields,
the river is rushing and the river is here.

The river of God sets our feet a-dancing,
the river of God fills our hearts with cheer,
the river of God fills our mouths with laughter,
and we rejoice for the river is here.

The river of God is teeming with life,
and all who touch it can be revived;
and those who linger on this river's shore
will come back thirsting for more of the Lord.

Up to the mountain we love to go
to find the presence of the Lord;
along the banks of the river we run,
we dance with laughter,
giving praise to the Son.

28

FAITHFUL ONE, so unchanging;
ageless One, you're my rock of peace.
Lord of all, I depend on you,
   I call out to you again and again,
   I call out to you again and again.

You are my rock in times of trouble,
you lift me up when I fall down;
all through the storm your love is the anchor –
my hope is in you alone.

28A

The Apostles' Creed
I believe in God, the Father almighty,
creator of heaven and earth. I believe in
Jesus Christ, his only Son, our Lord. He
was conceived by the power of the Holy
Spirit and born of the Virgin Mary. He
suffered under Pontius Pilate, was crucified,
died and was buried. On the third day he
rose again. He ascended into heaven, and is
seated at the right hand of the Father. He
will come again to judge the living and the
dead. I believe in the Holy Spirit, the holy
catholic Church, the communion of the
saints, the forgiveness of sins, the resurrection of the body, and the life everlasting.
Amen.

29

FAR AND NEAR hear the call,
worship him, Lord of all;
families of nations come
celebrate what God has done.

Say it loud, say it strong,
tell the world what God has done;
say it loud, praise his name,
let the earth rejoice – the Lord reigns.

Deep and wide is the love
heaven sent from above;
God's own Son, for sinners died,
rise again – he is alive.

At his name, let praise begin –
oceans roar, nature sings
for he comes to judge the earth
in righteousness and in his truth.

… the Lord reigns.

Graham Kendrick
Copyright © 1996 Make Way Music

30

FATHER GOD, fill this place with your love,
with your grace;
as we call on your name,
visit us in power again.

Spirit, come with your peace,
heal our wounds, bring release;
Lord, we long for your touch,
fill our hearts with your love.

Lord, we worship you;
Lord, we worship you.
Lord, we worship you …

Dave Bilbrough
Copyright © 1995 Kingsway's Thankyou Music

31

FATHER, HEAR OUR PRAYER
that our lives may be
consecrated only unto you.
Cleanse us with your fire,
fill us with your power
that the world may glorify your name.
Lord, have mercy on us.
Christ, have mercy on us.
Lord, have mercy on us.

Andy Piercy
Copyright © 1995 IQ Music

32

FATHER OF CREATION,
unfold your sovereign plan.
Raise up a chosen generation
that will march through the land.
All of creation is longing
for your unveiling of power –
would you release your anointing?
O God, let this be the hour!

Let your glory fall in this room,
let it go forth from here to the nations;
let your fragrance rest in this place
as we gather to seek your face.

Ruler of the nations,
the world has yet to see
the full release of your promise –
the church in victory.

continued over…

30A

from Psalm 105

Give thanks to the Lord, call on his name;
make hid deeds be known in the world around.

Sing to him, sing praise to him;
tell of the wonderful things he has done.

Glory in his holy name;
let those who seek the Lord rejoice!

Amen.

© ☥

31A

Before worship

O God, help us to remember that you
are here with us, to pray to you and sing
your praise with all our hearts, and, to
listen to your word with open ears;
through Jesus Christ our Lord.

Amen.

after C S Woodward from the Children's Service published by the
Society for Promoting Christian Knowledge

Turn to us, Lord, and touch us,
make us strong in your might;
overcome our weakness
that we may stand up and fight!

MEN   Let your kingdom come,
WOMEN   let your kingdom come,
MEN   let your will be done,
WOMEN   let your will be done,
MEN   let us see on earth,
WOMEN   let us see on earth,
ALL   the glory of your Son.

Let your glory fall in this place
let your glory fall in this place
let your glory fall in this place
let your glory fall in this place.

33

FOR THE JOYS AND
FOR THE SORROWS –
the best and worst of times,
for this moment, for tomorrow,
for all that lies behind;
fears that crowd around me,
for the failure of my plans,
for the dreams of all I hope
to be, the truth of what I am:

For this I have Jesus,
for this I have Jesus,
for this I have Jesus,
I have Jesus.

For the tears that flow in secret,
in the broken times,
for the moments of elation,
or the troubled mind;
for all the disappointments,
or the sting of old regrets –
all my prayers and longings,
that seem unanswered yet:

For the weakness of my body,
the burdens of each day,
for the nights of doubt and worry
when sleep has fled away;
needing reassurance
and the will to start again –
a steely-eyed endurance,
the strength to fight and win:

34

FROM WHERE THE SUN RISES,
even to the place it goes down –
we're giving you praise,
giving you praise.
From sun-kissed islands,
and even where the cold wind blows –
we're giving you praise,
giving you praise.

Even in the night when the sun goes down,
we're giving you praise;
passing it along as the world goes round,
we're giving you praise.

We're lifting our faces,
looking at the One we all love –
we're giving you praise,
giving you praise.
All colours and races joining
with the angels above –
we're giving you praise,
giving you praise.

35

GOD, BE GRACIOUS and bless us
and make your face shine on us:
let your ways be known,
your salvation shown
all over the earth;
let your ways be known,
your salvation shown
all over the earth.

May the peoples praise you, O God,
may all the peoples praise you;
may the nations be glad and sing for joy,
for you come to rule them justly.
May the peoples praise you, O God,
for you guide the nations of the earth;
may the peoples praise you, O God,
the nations be glad and sing for joy.

36

GOD IS GOOD ALL THE TIME!

he put a song of praise in
this heart of mine;
God is good all the time!
through the darkest night his light will shine:
God is good, God is good all the time!

If you're walking through the valley
and there are shadows all around,
do not fear, he will guide you,
he will keep you safe and sound
'cause he has promised to never leave you
nor forsake you, and his word is true.

We were sinners so unworthy,
still for us he chose to die:
filled us with his Holy Spirit,
now we can stand and testify
that his love is everlasting
and his mercies they will never end.

Though I may not understand
all the plans you have for me,
my life is in your hands,
and through the eyes of faith
I can clearly see:

> *... God is good, he's so good;*
> *God is good, he's so good;*
> *God is good, he's so good all the time!*

37

GOD IS HERE, GOD IS PRESENT,

God is moving by his Spirit:
will you hear what he is saying,
are you willing to respond?

God is here, God is present,
God is working by his Spirit:
Lord, I open up my life to you,
please do just what you want.

> *Lord, I won't stop loving you,*
> *you mean more to me than anything else;*
> *Lord, I won't stop loving you,*
> *you mean more to me than life itself.*

36A

Praise the Lord for creation

from Psalm 148

Praise the Lord:

Praise the Lord from the heavens:

(a) praise him
in the heights above.

Praise him, all his angels:

(b) praise him,
all his heavenly host.

Praise him, sun and moon:

(a) praise him,
all you shining stars.

Let them praise the name of the Lord:

(b) praise the Lord!

Praise the Lord from the earth:

(a) praise him,
great sea creatures.

Praise him, storms and clouds:

(b) praise him,
mountains and hills.

Praise him, fields and woods:

(a) praise him, animals and birds.

Praise him, rulers and nations:

(b) praise him, old and young.

Let them praise the name of the Lord:

(all) praise the Lord!
Amen.

© ✝

(the congregation may divide into two groups A & B.)

38

GREAT IS THE DARKNESS

that covers the earth,
oppression, injustice and pain;
nations are slipping in hopeless despair,
though many have come in your name –
watching while sanity dies,
touched by the madness and lies.

Come, Lord Jesus, come, Lord Jesus,
pour out your Spirit we pray;
come, Lord Jesus, come, Lord Jesus,
pour out your Spirit on us today.

May now your church rise with power and love,
this glorious gospel proclaim;
in every nation salvation will come
to those who believe in your name.
Help us bring light to this world,
that we might speed your return.

Great celebrations on that final day,
when out of the heavens you come;
darkness will vanish, all sorrow will end,
and rulers will bow at your throne;
our great commission complete,
then face to face we shall meet.

Noel Richards & Gerald Coates
Copyright © 1992 Kingsway's Thankyou Music

39

GREAT IS THE LORD

and most worthy of praise,
the city of our God, the holy place,
the joy of the whole earth.
Great is the Lord,
in whom we have the victory!
He aids us against the enemy –
we bow down on our knees.

And Lord, we want to lift your name on high,
and Lord, we want to thank you
for the works you've done in our lives;
and Lord, we trust in your unfailing love,
for you alone are God eternal
throughout earth and heaven above.

Steve McEwan
Copyright © 1985 Body Songs/CopyCare Ltd.

38A

Holy Spirit rule our hearts

Almighty God, without you we are
not able to please you. Mercifully
grant that your Holy Spirit may in all
things rule our hearts; through Jesus
Christ our Lord.

Amen.

Pentecost 6 Collect/© ASB 1980.

38B

Responsive Covenant

I am no longer my own, but yours.

Put me to what you will, rank me with
whom you will.

Put me to doing, put me to suffering.

Let me be employed for you, or laid
aside for you; exalted for you, or
brought low for you.

Let me be full, let me be empty; let me
have all things, let me have nothing.

I freely and gladly yield all things to your
pleasure and disposal.

And now, O glorious and blessed God,
Father, Son and Holy Spirit, you are
mine and I am yours.

So be it.

And the Covenant which I have made
on earth, let it be ratified in heaven.

Amen.

© Taken from The Covenant Service
Methodist Book of Offices

40

GREAT IS YOUR FAITHFULNESS,
O God my Father,
you have fulfilled all your promise to me;
you never fail and your love is unchanging –
all you have been, you for ever will be.

*Great is your faithfulness,
   great is your faithfulness,
morning by morning new mercies I see;
all I have needed your hand has provided –
great is your faithfulness, Father, to me.*

Summer and winter and springtime and harvest,
sun, moon and stars in their courses above
join with all nature in eloquent witness
to your great faithfulness, mercy and love.

Pardon for sin, and a peace everlasting,
your living presence to cheer and to guide;
strength for today and bright hope for tomorrow –
these are the blessings your love will provide.

41

HAVE YOU HEARD
THE GOOD NEWS,
*have you heard the good news?
We can live in hope
because of what the Lord has done.
Have you heard …*

There is a way
when there seems no other way,
there is a light in the darkness;
there is a hope, an everlasting hope,
there is a God who can help us.

A hope for justice
and a hope for peace,
a hope for those in desperation:
we have a future if only we believe
he works in every situation.

43A

Luke 24:5, 6

'Why do you look for the living
amongst the dead?

He is not here; he has risen!'

42

HE BROUGHT ME TO
HIS BANQUETING TABLE,

MEN	He brought me
WOMEN	He brought me to his banqueting table,
MEN	he brought me to his banqueting table;
WOMEN	he brought me to his banqueting table;
ALL	and his banner over me is love.
MEN	I am my belovèd's and he is mine,
WOMEN	I am my belovèd's and he is mine,
MEN	yes, I am my belovèd's and he is mine;
WOMEN	I am my belovèd's and he is mine;
ALL	and his banner over me is love, yes, his banner over me is love.
ALL	And we can feel the love of God in this place: we believe your goodness, we receive your grace; we delight ourselves at your table, O God, you do all things well – just look at our lives.

43

HE HAS RISEN,
*he has risen,
he has risen,
Jesus is alive.*

When the life flowed from his body –
seemed like Jesus' mission failed,
but his sacrifice accomplished
victory over sin and hell.

In the grave God did not leave him
for his body to decay;
raised to life – the great awakening –
Satan's power he overcame.

If there were no resurrection,
we ourselves could not be raised;
but the Son of God is living
so our hope is not in vain.

When the Lord rides out of heaven,
mighty angels at his side,
they will sound the final trumpet –
from the grave we shall arise. *continued over…*

He has given life immortal,
we shall see him face to face;
through eternity we'll praise him,
Christ the champion of our faith.

44

HE IS EXALTED,

the King is exalted on high –
I will praise him;
he is exalted, for ever exalted –
and I will praise his name!
He is the Lord;
for ever his truth shall reign;
heaven and earth
rejoice in his holy name.
He is exalted, the King is exalted on high!

45

HE IS THE LORD, and he reigns on high –

he is the Lord;
spoke into the darkness, created the light –
he is the Lord;
who is like unto him, never ending in days?
he is the Lord.
And he comes in power when
we call on his name –
he is the Lord!
Show your power, O Lord our God;
show your power, O Lord our God, our God!

Your gospel, O Lord, is the hope for our nation –
you are the Lord;
it's the power of God for our salvation,
you are the Lord;
we ask not for riches, but look to the cross:
you are the Lord.
And for our inheritance give us the lost –
you are the Lord!
Send your power, O Lord our God;
send your power, O Lord our God, our God!

He is the Lord …

46

HE'S GIVEN ME A GARMENT OF PRAISE

instead of a spirit of despair;
he's given me a garment of praise
instead of a spirit of despair.

He's given me …

A crown of beauty instead of ashes,
the oil of gladness instead of mourning –
my soul rejoices as I delight myself in God.

He's given me …

47

WOMEN	**HEAR OUR CRY,** O hear our cry:
MEN	'Jesus, come!'
WOMEN	Hear our cry, O hear our cry:
MEN	'Jesus, come!'

The tide of prayer is rising,
a deeper passion burning –
WOMEN   Hear our cry …
We lift our eyes with longing
to see your kingdom coming –
WOMEN   Hear our cry …

WOMEN   Whoever is thirsty,
come now and drink the waters
of life;
MEN   whoever is thirsty,
come now and drink the waters
of life.
WOMEN   Hear our cry, O hear our cry:

47A

Assurance Of Forgiveness

May God, our heavenly Father, who has
promised to forgive all those who sincerely
turn to him, have mercy on each one of
you, deliver you from your sins, and
strengthen you for his service: through
Jesus Christ our Lord.

Amen.

© ℗

MEN   'Jesus, come!'
WOMEN   Hear our cry, O hear our cry:
MEN   'Jesus, come!'

The streets of teeming cities
cry out for healing rivers –
WOMEN   Hear our cry …
Refresh them with your presence,
give grace for deep repentance –
WOMEN   Hear our cry …

WOMEN   Whoever is thirsty …

Tear back the shroud of shadows
that covers all the peoples –
WOMEN   Hear our cry …
Revealing your salvation
in every tribe and nation –
WOMEN   Hear our cry …

WOMEN   Whoever is thirsty …

Graham Kendrick
Copyright © 1996 Make Way Music

48

HERE IS LOVE vast as the ocean,
loving kindness as the flood,
when the Prince of life, our ransom,
shed for us his precious blood.
Who his love will not remember;
who can cease to sing his praise?
He can never be forgotten
throughout heaven's eternal days.

On the mount of crucifixion
fountains opened deep and wide;
through the floodgates of God's mercy
flowed a vast and gracious tide.
Grace and love, like mighty rivers,
poured incessant from above;
and heaven's peace and perfect justice
kissed a guilty world in love.

After William Rees, William Edwards

49

HERE WE STAND
IN TOTAL SURRENDER,
lifting our voices, abandoned to your cause;
here we stand, praying in the glory
of the one and only Jesus Christ, the Lord.

This time – revival;
Lord, come and heal our land,
bring to completion

the work that you've begun.
This time – revival;
stir up your church again,
pour out your Spirit
on your daughters and your sons.

Here we stand in need of your mercy –
Father, forgive us for the time
that we have lost.
Once again make us an army
to conquer this nation
with the message of the cross.

Charlie Groves & Andy Piercy
© 1995 IQ Music

50

HOLY, HOLY, HOLY,
holy, holy, holy,
holy is the Lord God almighty!
Worthy to receive glory,
worthy to receive honour,
worthy to receive all our praise today.

Praise him, praise him and lift him up;
Praise him, exalt his name for ever.
Praise him, praise him and lift him up;
Praise him, exalt his name for ever.

Gary Oliver
Copyright © 1991 Highest Praise Publishing/CopyCare

51

HOLY, HOLY, HOLY,
LORD GOD ALMIGHTY!
Early in the morning our song of praise shall be:
Holy, holy, holy! – merciful and mighty,
God in three persons, glorious Trinity.

continued over…

51A

Ephesians 2:8-10

For it is by grace you have been saved,
through faith—and this not from
yourselves, it is the gift of God not by
works, so that no-one can boast. For
we are God's workmanship, created in
Christ Jesus to do good works, which
God prepared in advance for us to do.

Holy, holy, holy! All the saints adore you
casting down their royal crowns
      around the glassy sea,
cherubim and seraphim falling down before you:
you were and are, and evermore shall be!

Holy, holy, holy! Though the darkness hide you,
though the sinful human eye
      your glory may not see,
you alone are holy, there is none beside you,
perfect in power, in love and purity.

Holy, holy, holy, Lord God almighty!
All your works shall praise your name,
      in earth and sky and sea:
Holy, holy, holy! – merciful and mighty,
God in three persons, glorious Trinity.

Reginald Heber
© in this version Jubilate Hymns

52

HOLY JESUS, burn your fire in me,
Holy Jesus, sanctify;
Holy Jesus, full of grace and mercy,
Holy Jesus, we lift you high.

Son of God, Word of God,
fill me up with your love;
Son of God, Word of God,
fill me up with your love –
with your love, with your love,
with your love, with your love.

Ian Mizen and Andy Pressdee
Copyright © 1994 Brown Bear Music

53

HOLY ONE, my life is in your hand,
my song an offering of my heart;
redeemed, washed clean,
by faith I stand secure –
in you, Jesus, I live.

    To you the glory,
    to you the power,
    to you the honour for evermore;
    your love brings healing,
    your love's eternal,
    your love's the answer,
    the hope of the world,
    the hope of the world.

Mick Gisbey
Copyright © 1993 Kingsway's Thankyou Music

54

HOW DEEP THE FATHER'S LOVE FOR US,

how vast beyond all measure,
that he should give his only Son
to make a wretch his treasure.
How great the pain of searing loss:
the Father turns his face away
as wounds which mar the chosen one
bring many sons to glory.

Behold the man upon a cross,
my sin upon his shoulders;
ashamed, I hear my mocking voice
call out among the scoffers.
It was my sin that held him there
until it was accomplished;
his dying breath has brought me life –
I know that it is finished.

I will not boast in anything,
no gifts, no power, no wisdom;
but I will boast in Jesus Christ,
his death and resurrection.
Why should I gain from his reward?
I cannot give an answer,
but this I know with all my heart,
his wounds have paid my ransom.

Stuart Townend
Copyright © 1995 Kingsway's Thankyou Music

55

HOW GOOD AND HOW PLEASANT IT IS

when we all live in unity –
refreshing as dew at the dawn,
like rare anointing oil upon the head.

    It's so good, so good
    when we live together
    in peace and harmony;
    it's so good, so good
    when we live together in his love.

How deep are the rivers that run
when we are one in Jesus
and share with the Father and Son
the blessings of his everlasting life.

From Psalm 133
Graham Kendrick
Copyright © 1995 Make Way Music

56

HOW WONDERFUL, *how glorious*
is the love of God,
bringing healing, forgiveness –
wonderful love!

Let celebration echo through this land:
we bring reconciliation,
we bring hope to every one.

We proclaim the kingdom of our God is here:
come and join the heavenly anthem
ringing loud and ringing clear.

Listen to the music as his praises fill the air;
with joy and with gladness
tell the people everywhere:

Dave Bilbrough
Copyright © 1994 Kingsway's Thankyou Music

56A

Prayer of dedication

Eternal God, you have declared in
Christ the completion of your purpose
of love. May we live by faith, walk in
hope, and be renewed in love, until the
world reflects your glory, and you are
all in all. Even so, come, Lord Jesus.

Amen.

© ASB 1980.

57

I BELIEVE, I BELIEVE, I BELIEVE;
I believe, I believe, I believe;
I believe, I believe, I believe,
I believe, I believe.

I believe in God, the Father almighty,
I believe that he made the earth and heavens;
I believe in Jesus, born of a woman,
I believe that he is the Son of God.

I believe in Jesus, teacher and healer,
I believe that his life was poor and simple;
I believe he died betrayed and rejected,
I believe that he fought the power of evil.

I believe the holy life-giving Spirit
is a gift of the Son and Father to us;
I believe the three are one and united,
I believe in his healing and forgiveness.

I believe that Jesus died and was buried,
I believe that he rose to life again;
I believe that he was taken to heaven,
I believe that he reigns at God's right hand.

I believe that he will come back in glory,
I believe he will judge the dead and living;
I believe the resurrection of body,
I believe in the life that's everlasting.

Andy Thornton & Doug Gay
Copyright © 1995 Andy Thornton/Sticky Music

58

I GIVE YOU ALL THE HONOUR
and praise that's due your name:
for you are the King of glory,
the creator of all things.

And I worship you, I give my life to you,
I fall down on my knees;
yes, I worship you, I give my life to you,
I fall down on my knees.

As your Spirit moves upon me now,
you meet my deepest need;
and I lift my hands up to your throne –
your mercy I've received.

You have broken chains that bound me,
you've set this captive free;
I will lift my voice to praise your name
for all eternity.

From 1 Chronicles 16 and Luke 4 Carl Tuttle
Copyright © 1982 Mercy/Vineyard Publishing /Music Services/CopyCare

---

59

I JUST WANT TO BE
WHERE YOU ARE,
dwelling daily in your presence;
I don't want to worship from afar:
draw me near to where you are.

I just want to be where you are,
in your dwelling place for ever;
take me to the place where you are:
I just want to be with you.

continued over…

I want to be where you are,
dwelling in your presence,
feasting at your table,
surrounded by your glory –
in your presence,
     that's where I always want to be:
I just want to be, I just want to be with you.

I just want to be where you are,
to enter boldly in your presence;
I don't want to worship from afar:
draw me near to where you are.

O my God, you are my strength and my song,
and when I'm in your presence
     though I'm weak, you're always strong.

I just want to be where you are,
in your dwelling place for ever,
take me to the place where you are:
I just want to be, I just want to be with you;
I just want to be, I just want to be with you.

Don Moen
Copyright © 1989 Integrity's Hosanna! Music/Integrity Music Europe

60

I SEE THE LORD seated on the throne
   – exalted;
and the train of his robe
fills the temple with glory:
the whole earth is filled,
the whole earth is filled,
the whole earth is filled
with your glory.

Holy, holy, holy, holy,
yes, holy is the Lord;
holy, holy, holy, holy,
yes, holy is the Lord of lords.

Chris Falson (From Isaiah 6)
Copyright ©1993 Chris Falson Music/Maranatha! Music/CopyCare Ltd.

61

I WALK BY FAITH,

each step by faith;
to live by faith
I put my trust in you.

Every step I take is a step of faith –
no weapon formed against me shall prosper.
And every prayer I make is a prayer of faith –
and if my God is for me
     then who can be against me?

Chris Falson
Copyright © 1990 Chris Falson Music/Maranatha! Music/CopyCare Ltd.

62

I WANT TO BE A TREE that's bearing fruit,
that God has pruned and caused to shoot,
oh, up in the sky so very, very high –
I want to be, I want to be a blooming tree.

God has promised his Holy Spirit
will water our roots and help us grow;
listen and obey, and before you know it,
your fruit will start to grow,
grow,
   grow,
     grow,
       grow!

You'll be a tree that's bearing fruit,
with a very, very, very strong root;
bright colours like daisies,
more fruit than Sainsbury's –
you'll be a blooming tree.

God has promised his Holy Spirit
will water our roots and make them grow;
listen and obey, and before you know it,
your fruit will start to grow,
grow,
   grow,
     grow,
       grow!

You'll be a blooming tree,
you'll be a blooming tree!

Doug Horley
Copyright © 1996 Kingsway's Thankyou Music

63

I WANT TO BE OUT OF
MY DEPTH IN YOUR LOVE,

feeling your arms so strong around me;
out of my depth in your love,
out of my depth in you.

Learning to let you lead,
putting all trust in you;
deeper into your arms,
surrounded by you.

Things I have held so tight,
made my security;
give me the strength I need –
to simply let go.

Doug Horley
Copyright © 1995 Kingsway's Thankyou Music

64

I WILL DANCE, I will sing,
to be mad for my King;
nothing, Lord, is hindering
the passion in my soul.

I will dance ...

And I'll become
even more undignified than this;
some would say it's foolishness,
but I'll become
even more undignified than this.

And I'll become ...

Na, na, na, na, na – hey! (x 7)

Here I,
here I,
here I,
here I go.

Matt Redman
Copyright © 1995 Kingsway's Thankyou Music

65

I WILL OFFER UP MY LIFE

in spirit and truth,
pouring out the oil of love
as my worship to you.
In surrender I must give
my every part:
Lord, receive the sacrifice
of a broken heart.

*Jesus, what can I give,
what can I bring
to so faithful a friend,
to so loving a king?
Saviour, what can be said,
what can be sung
as a praise of your name
for the things you have done?
Oh, my words could not tell,
not even in part,*

*of the debt of love that is owed
by this thankful heart.*

You deserve my every breath,
for you've paid the great cost –
giving up your life to death,
even death on a cross.
You took all my shame away,
there defeated my sin,
opened up the gates of heaven
and have beckoned me in.

Jesus, what can I give, ...

*What can I give, what can I bring,
what can I sing as an offering, Lord?
What can I give ...*

Matt Redman
Copyright © 1993 Kingsway's Thankyou Music

66

I WILL WORSHIP (I will worship)
with all of my heart (with all of my heart);
I will praise you (I will praise you)
with all of my strength (all my strength).
I will seek you (I will seek you)
all of my days (all of my days);
I will follow (I will follow)
all of your ways (all your ways).

*I will give you all my worship,
I will give you all my praise;
you alone I long to worship,
you alone are worthy of my praise.*

I will bow down (I will bow down) –
hail you as king (hail you as king);

continued over...

I will serve you (I will serve you),
give you everything (everything);
I will lift up (I will lift up)
my eyes to your throne
     (my eyes to your throne);
I will trust you (I will trust you),
I will trust you alone (trust you alone).

David Ruis
© 1993 Mercy/Vineyard Publishing/Music Services/CopyCare

67

I WORSHIP YOU, ALMIGHTY GOD,

there is none like you;
I worship you, O Prince of Peace –
that is what I love to do.
I give you praise,
for you are my righteousness;
I worship you, almighty God,
there is none like you.

Sandra Corbett
Copyright © 1983 Integrity's Hosanna! Music
/Integrity Music Europe

68

I'M GOING TO BUILD MY HOUSE

on solid rock,
going to build my house on solid rock,
so I won't wake up to a nasty shock
to find nothing but a pile of rubble.

Don't want to build a house
    on foundations that will wobble,
don't want to build a house with any dodgy bricks;
don't want to build a house that will
    shake like a jelly,
I want to shout out loud:
'Of this house you can be proud!'

Jesus said, 'Take my words and
    put them into action;
make these words,' he said,
    'foundations in your life.'
Build with care or else your
    house will surely tumble,
and it's not a clever trick to own a pile of bricks.

Jesus said, 'Take my words and
    put them into action;
make these words,' he said,
    'foundations in your life.'
And when the river comes and
    crashes up against you,
you won't get washed away –
instead you'll cheer and say:

Based on Matthew 7 Doug Horley
Copyright © 1996 Kingsway's Thankyou Music

69

IMMORTAL, INVISIBLE, God only wise,

in light inaccessible hid from our eyes;
most holy, most glorious, the ancient of days,
almighty, victorious, your great name we praise.

Unresting, unhasting, and silent as light,
nor wanting, nor wasting, you rule us in might;
your justice like mountains high soaring above,
your clouds which are fountains
    of goodness and love.

To all you are giving, to life great and small,
in all you are living, the true life of all:
we blossom and flourish, uncertain and frail,
we wither and perish, but you never fail.

We worship before you, great Father of light,
while angels adore you, all veiling their sight;
our praises we render, O Father, to you
whom only the splendour of light hides from view.

Walter Smith
© in the version Jubilate Hymns

70

IS IT TRUE TODAY that when people pray

Cloudless skies will break,
kings and queens will shake?
Yes, it's true and I believe it,
I'm living for you.

Is it true today that when people pray
we'll see dead men rise
and the blind set free?
Yes, it's true and I believe it,
I'm living for you.

I'm going to be a history-maker in this land.
I'm going to be a speaker of truth to all mankind.
I'm going to stand, I'm going to run
into your arms, into your arms again:
into your arms, into your arms again.

Yes, it's true today that when people stand
with the fire of God, with the truth in hand,
we'll see miracles, we'll see angels sing,
we'll see broken hearts making history.
Yes, it's true and we believe it,
we're living for you.

Martin Smith
© 1996 Curious? Music UK/Kingsway's Thankyou Music

71

IT'S GOOD TO BE HUMAN –

good to be alive,
living in your world;
thanks for life!
Such incredible diversity –
it's good to be alive:
thanks for the gift –
thanks for life!
Celebrating wonder, mystery, awe and beauty,
a sense of the profound;
thanks for life – it's a gift from you!

The whole world is your throne –
it's good to be alive;
singing out a song of praise:
thanks for life!
You've unleashed such creativity –
it's good to be alive;
thanks for the gift –
thanks for life!
Shaking off our numbness,
savouring pleasure – the ecstasy of living:
thanks for life – it's a gift from you!

Jon Baker
Copyright © 1995 Serious Music UK

71A

I Peter 2:9

You are a chosen people, a royal
priesthood, a holy nation, a people
belonging to God, that you may declare
the praises of him who called you out
of darkness into his marvellous light.

72

IT'S OUR CONFESSION, Lord, that we

are weak,
so very weak, but you are strong;
and though we've nothing, Lord,
to lay at your feet,
we come to your feet and say: 'Help us along.'
It's our confession …

A broken heart and a contrite spirit
you have yet to deny;
your heart of mercy beats with
love's strong current –
let the river flow by your Spirit now, Lord.
We cry:

'Let your mercies fall from heaven,
sweet mercies flow from heaven,
new mercies for today:
O shower them down, Lord, as we pray.'
David Ruis © 1995 Mercy/Vineyard Publishing
/Music Services/CopyCare

73

IT'S RISING UP from coast to coast,

from north to south, and east to west;
the cry of hearts that love your name,
which with one voice we will proclaim.

The former things have taken place:
can this be the new day of praise –
a heavenly song that comes to birth
and reaches out to all the earth?

O, let the cry to nations ring
that all may come and all may sing
'Holy is the Lord,
'holy is the Lord,
'holy is the Lord,
'holy is the Lord!'

And we have heard the Lion's roar
that speaks of heaven's love and power:
is this the time, is this the call
that ushers in your kingdom rule?

O, let the cry to nations ring,
that all may come and all may sing:
'Jesus is alive,
'Jesus is alive,
'Jesus is alive,
'Jesus is alive!'

Matt Redman & Martin Smith
Copyright © 1995 Kingsway's Thankyou Music

74

JESUS CHRIST, I think upon your sacrifice:

you became nothing, poured out to death.
Many times I've wondered at your gift of life,
and I'm in that place once again,
I'm in that place once again.

And once again I look upon
the cross where you died:
I'm humbled by your mercy and
I'm broken inside,
once again I thank you,
once again I pour out my life.

continued over...

Now you are exalted to the highest place –
King of the heavens – where one day I'll bow,
but for now, I marvel at this saving grace,
and I'm full of praise once again,
I'm full of praise once again.

75

JESUS, GOD'S RIGHTEOUSNESS REVEALED,

the Son of Man, the Son of God –
his kingdom comes;
Jesus, redemption's sacrifice,
now glorified, now justified –
his kingdom comes.

And this kingdom will know no end,
and its glory shall know no bounds,
for the majesty and power
of this kingdom's king has come;
and this kingdom's reign, and this kingdom's rule,
and this kingdom's power and authority –
Jesus, God's righteousness revealed.

Jesus, the expression of God's love,
the grace of God,
the word of God revealed to us;
Jesus, God's holiness displayed,
now glorified, now justified –
his kingdom comes.

76

JESUS IS KING, and we will extol him,

give him the glory and honour his name;
he reigns on high, enthroned in the heavens –
Word of the Father, exalted for us.

We have a hope that is steadfast and certain,
gone through the curtain and touching the throne;
we have a Priest who is there interceding,
pouring his grace on our lives day by day.

We come to him our Priest and Apostle,
clothed in his glory and bearing his name,
laying our lives with gladness before him –
filled with his Spirit we worship the King:

'O Holy One, our hearts do adore you;
thrilled with your goodness,
    we give you our praise!'
Angels in light with worship surround him,
Jesus, our Saviour, for ever the same.

75A

Deuteronomy 6:5-7

Love the Lord your God with all your heart and with all your soul and with all your strength. These commandments that I give you today are to be upon your hearts. Impress them on your children. Talk about them when you sit at home and when you walk down the road, when you lie down and when you get up.

75B

Prayer of Humble Access

We do not presume to come to your table, merciful Lord, trusting in our own righteousness, but in your manifold and great mercies. We are not worthy so much as to gather up the crumbs under your table. But you are the same Lord whose nature is always to have mercy. Grant us therefore, gracious Lord, so to eat the flesh of your dear Son Jesus Christ and to drink his blood, that we may evermore dwell in him and he in us.

Amen.

77

JESUS IS THE NAME WE HONOUR,

Jesus is the name we praise.
Majestic name above all other names;
the highest heaven and earth proclaim
    that Jesus is our God.

We will glorify, we will lift him high,
we will give him honour and praise.
We will glorify, we will lift him high,
we will give him honour and praise.

Jesus is the name we worship,
Jesus is the name we trust.
He is the King above all other kings;
let all creation stand and sing
   that Jesus is our God.

Jesus is the Father's splendour,
Jesus is the Father's joy.
He will return to reign in majesty,
and every eye at last shall see
   that Jesus is our God.

Phil Lawson-Johnston
Copyright © 1991 Kingsway's Thankyou Music

78

JESUS, JESUS, HOLY AND ANOINTED ONE, JESUS.

Jesus, Jesus,
risen and exalted One, Jesus:
   your name is like honey on my lips,
your Spirit like water to my soul;
your word is a lamp unto my feet –
Jesus, I love you, I love you.

John Barnett Copyright © 1985 Mercy/Vineyard Publishing
/Music Services/CopyCare

79

JESUS' LOVE HAS GOT UNDER OUR SKIN;

Jesus' love has got under our skin –
Jesus' love has got under our skin;
Jesus' love has got under our skin –
deeper than colour, oh,
richer than culture, oh,
stronger than emotion, oh,
wider than the ocean, oh!
Don't you want to celebrate
and congratulate somebody?
Talk about a family!
It's under our skin,
under our skin.

LEADER   Everybody say love:
ALL   love.
LEADER   Everybody say love:
ALL   love,
LEADER   love,
ALL   love!

Isn't it good to be living in harmony –
Jesus in you and me?
He's under our skin,
under our skin;
he's under our skin,
under our skin.

Graham Kendrick Copyright © 1996 Make Way Music

80

JESUS, LOVER OF MY SOUL,

all consuming fire is in your gaze;
Jesus, I want you to know
I will follow you all my days
for no one else in history is like you,
and history itself belongs to you.
Alpha and Omega, you have loved me,
and I will share eternity with you.

It's all about you, Jesus,
and all this is for you,
for your glory and your fame;
it's not about me,
as if you should do things my way –
you alone are God
and I surrender to your ways.

Paul Oakley Copyright © 1995 Kingsway's Thankyou Music

81

JOY TO THE WORLD! The Lord has come:
let earth receive her king,
let every heart prepare him room
and heaven and nature sing,
and heaven and nature sing,
and heaven, and heaven and nature sing.

He rules the world with truth and grace,
and makes the nations prove
the glories of his righteousness,
the wonders of his love,
the wonders of his love,
the wonders, wonders of his love.

Isaac Watts © 1996 Make Way Music

82

LET THE HEAVENS REJOICE *and*
   the earth be glad,
   let the seas resound with a mighty roar;
   let the trees of the forest clap their hands,
   let the earth be filled with the glory of the Lord.

All of creation is boldly proclaiming
the wonderful things he has done;
let's join with all nations in one declaration,
proclaiming the goodness of God.

The heavens above are declaring his splendour –
his power cannot be denied,
for all of creation is loudly confessing
that Jesus, our Lord, is alive.

Don Harris and Martin J Nystrom (From Psalm 96) Copyright ©
1993 Integrity's Hosanna! Music/Integrity Music Europe

83

LET US RUN WITH PERSEVERANCE

the race set out before us;
let us fix our eyes on Jesus,
the author and perfecter of our faith.

In the beginning the Word was with God,
through him all of us were made;
he began a work in us, a good work
to perfect until he returns again.

Since we are surrounded by
heaven's cheering crowd,
let us throw off every chain:
for all that oppresses us, look to Jesus
who endured
so we'll not lose heart again.

For the joy before him, he suffered the cross,
he defeated death and shame,
now he reigns in glory at the right hand of God –
he is calling us by name.

From Hebrews 12 David Lyle Morris
Copyright © 1996 Tevita Music

84

LORD, I COME TO YOU,

let my heart be changed, renewed,
flowing from the grace that I found in you.
And, Lord, I've come to know
the weaknesses I see in me
will be stripped away
by the power of your love.

Hold me close, let your love surround me,
bring me near, draw me to your side;
and as I wait, I'll rise up like the eagle,
and I will soar with you;
your Spirit leads me on
in the power of your love.

Lord, unveil my eyes,
let me see you face to face,
the knowledge of your love,
as you live in me.
Lord, renew my mind
as your will unfolds in my life,
in living every day in the power of your love.

Geoff Bullock Copyright © 1992 Word Music Incl
Word Music (UK)/CopyCare Ltd

85

LORD, I LIFT YOUR NAME ON HIGH,

Lord, I love to sing your praises;
I'm so glad you're in my life,
I'm so glad you came to save us.

You came from heaven to earth to show the way,
from the earth to the cross, my debt to pay;
from the cross to the grave,
from the grave to the sky,
Lord, I lift your name on high.

Rick Founds
Copyright © 1989 Maranatha! Music/CopyCare Ltd.

86

LORD, YOU HAVE SEARCHED ME

and you know me.
You know when I sit, you know when I rise.
You hem me in – behind and before,
and you have laid your hand on me.
If I go up to the heavens you are there;
and if I make my bed in the depths
you are there,
even there your right hand will hold me fast.

Search me, O God, and know my heart;
test me and know my anxious thoughts
and lead me, and lead me in the everlasting way.

From Psalm 139 Jonny Sutherland
Copyright © 1996 Serious Music UK

86A

Opening prayer

We have come together as the family
of God in our Father's presence to
offer him praise and thanksgiving, to
hear and receive his holy word, to
bring before him the needs of the
world, to ask his forgiveness of our
sins, and to seek his grace, that
through his Son Jesus Christ we may
give ourselves to his service.

Amen.

© ASB 1980.

87

LORD, YOU HAVE MY HEART,

and I will search for yours:
Jesus, take my life and lead me on.

Lord, you have my heart,
and I will search for yours:
let me be to you a sacrifice.

MEN	And I will praise you, Lord,
WOMEN	I will praise you, Lord,
MEN	and I will sing of love come down,
WOMEN	I will sing of love come down,
MEN	and as you show your face,
WOMEN	show your face,
ALL	we'll see your glory here.

Martin Smith
Copyright © 1992 Kingsway's Thankyou Music

88

LOVE SONGS FROM HEAVEN are

filling the earth,
bringing great hope to all nations;
evil has prospered, but truth is alive –
in this dark world, the light still shines.

Nothing has silenced this gospel of Christ;
it echoes down through the ages.
Blood of the martyrs
has made your church strong –
in this dark world, the light still shines.

For you we live and for you we may die,
through us may Jesus be seen;
for you alone we will offer our lives –
in this dark world, our light will shine.

Let every nation be filled with your song;
this is the cry of your people,
'we will not settle for anything less –
in this dark world, our light must shine.'

Noel & Tricia Richards
Copyright © 1996 Kingsway's Thankyou Music

89

MEN OF FAITH, rise up and sing

of the great and glorious King:
you are strong when you feel weak,
in your brokenness complete.

Shout to the north and the south,
sing to the east and the west:
'Jesus is saviour to all,
Lord of heaven and earth.'
Shout to the north ...

Rise up, women of the truth,
stand and sing to broken hearts:
who can know the healing power
of our glorious King of love?

We've been through fire,
we've been through rain;
we've been refined
by the power of his name.
We've fallen deeper in love with you –
you've burned the truth on our lips.

Rise up, church with broken wings,
fill this place with songs, again,
of our God who reigns on high:
by his grace, again we'll fly.

Shout to the north ...
... Lord of heaven and earth,
Lord of heaven and earth.

Martin Smith Copyright © 1995
Curious? Music UK/Kingsway's Thankyou Music

89A

Easter Greeting

We are risen with Christ –
the Lord is risen!
Eternal life is ours –
the Lord is risen!
Death has met its master –
the Lord is risen!
The way to heaven is open –
the Lord is risen!
He is risen indeed –
Alleluia! Amen.

© Frank Colquhoun, adapted ☩

90

MORE THAN OXYGEN, I need your love,

more than life-giving food the hungry dream of;
more than an eloquent word
depends on the tongue,
more than a passionate song needs to be sung.

More than a word could ever say,
more than a song could ever convey;
I need you more than all of these things,
Father, I need you more.

continued over...

More than magnet and steel are drawn to unite,
more than poets love words to rhyme as
    they write;
more than the comforting warmth of sun in
    the spring,
more than the eagle loves wind under its wings.

More than a blazing fire on a winter's night,
more than the tall evergreens reach for the light;
more than the pounding waves long for the shore,
more than these gifts you give, I love you more.

*Brian Doerkson Copyright © 1994 Mercy
/Vineyard Publishing/Music Services/CopyCare*

89B

Keeping
Jesus' Commandments

from Matthew 22 and John 13

We pray for God's strength to keep
Jesus' commandment:

'Love the Lord your God with all your
heart, with all your mind, with all your
soul, and with all your strength':

Lord, help us to obey. Amen.

'Love your neighbour as yourself':

Lord, help us to obey. Amen.

'Love one another as I have loved
you':

Lord, help us to obey.

In your mercy strengthen us and move
our hearts to do your will.

Amen.

© ℣

91

MY HEART WILL SING to you because of
        your great love,
a love so rich, so pure –
a love beyond compare;
the wilderness, the barren place
become a blessing in the warmth
of your embrace.

When earthly wisdom dims the light of knowing you
or if my search for understanding clouds your way,
to you I fly, my hiding place,
where revelation is beholding face to face.

---

*May my heart sing your praise for ever,
may my voice lift your name, my God;
may my soul know no other treasure
than your love, than your love.*

Robin Mark Copyright © 1996 Daybreak Music

92

MY HEART IS FULL of admiration
for you, my Lord, my God and King;
your excellence, my inspiration,
your words of grace
have made my spirit sing.

You love what's right and hate all evil;
therefore your God sets you on high;
and on your head pours oil of gladness,
while fragance fills your royal palaces.

*All the glory, honour and power
belong to you, belong to you;
Jesus, Saviour, anointed One,
I worship you, I worship you.*

Your throne, O God, will last for ever;
justice will be your royal decree:
in majesty, ride out victorious
for righteousness, truth and humility.

*From Hebrews 1 Graham Kendrick
Copyright © 1991 Make Way Music*

92A

Ephesians 4:4-6

There is one body, and one Spirit, Just
as you were called to one hope when
you were called, one Lord, one faith,
one baptism; one God and Father of all,
who is over all, and through all and in
all.

93

MY JESUS I LOVE THEE, I know thou
        art mine;
for thee, all the follies of sin I resign.
My gracious Redeemer, my saviour art thou,
if ever I loved thee, my Jesus 'tis now.

I love thee because thou has first loved me
and purchased my pardon on Calvary's tree.
I love thee for wearing the thorns on thy brow –
if ever I loved thee, my Jesus tis now.

In mansions of glory an endless delight,
I'll ever adore thee in heaven so bright.
I'll sing with the glittering crown on my brow,
'if ever I loved thee, my Jesus tis now.'

William R Featherstone

93A

Isaiah 56:1

Maintain justice and do what is right, for my salvation is close at hand and my righteousness will soon be revealed.

94

MY JESUS, MY SAVIOUR,

Lord, there is none like you;
all of my days I want to praise
the wonders of your mighty love.

My comfort, my shelter,
tower of refuge and strength,
let every breath, all that I am,
never cease to worship you.

Shout to the Lord all the earth,
let us sing power and majesty,
praise to the king:
mountains bow down and the seas will roar
at the sound of your name.

I sing for joy at the work of your hands –
for ever I'll love you, for ever I'll stand;
nothing compares to the promise
I have in you.

Shout to the Lord ...

Darlene Zschech

95

MY LIPS SHALL PRAISE YOU,

my great Redeemer;
my heart will worship,
almighty Saviour.

You take all my guilt away,
turn the darkest night to brightest day:
you are the restorer of my soul.

Love that conquers every fear!
In the midst of trouble you draw near:
you are the restorer of my soul.

You're the source of happiness,
bringing peace when I am in distress:
you are the restorer of my soul.

... almighty Saviour, almighty Saviour,
almighty Saviour!

Noel & Tricia Richards

95A

Praise
from Psalm 8

O Lord, our Lord,

how glorious is your name in all the earth!

High above the heavens your majesty is praised.

Amen.

© ℣

96

MY REDEEMER LIVES,

and I will see his glory
as he works all things together for my good –
whatever things occur, of this I can be sure:
I know my Redeemer lives.

Even though I walk through the valley,
I will fear no evil,
he is with me;
and on the battlefield, although the pain is real,
my struggles soon will fade
as his glory is revealed.

... I know my Redeemer lives;
I know my Redeemer lives.

Eugene Greco

97

MY SONG IS LOVE UNKNOWN,
my Saviour's love for me;
love to the loveless shown
that they might lovely be:
but who am I, that for my sake
my Lord should take frail flesh and die?

He came from heaven's throne
salvation to bestow;
but men refused, and none
the longed-for Christ would know:
this is my friend, my friend indeed,
who at my need his life did spend.

Sometimes they crowd his way
and his sweet praises sing,
resounding all the day
hosannas to their king;
then 'crucify' is all their breath,
and for his death they thirst and cry.

Why, what has my Lord done
to cause this rage and spite?
He made the lame to run,
and gave the blind their sight:
what injuries! yet these are why
the Lord most high so cruelly dies.

With angry shouts, they have
my dear Lord done away;
a murderer they save,
the Prince of Life they slay!
Yet willingly he bears the shame
that through his name all may be free.

In life no house, no home,
my Lord on earth may have;
in death no friendly tomb
but what a stranger gave.
What may I say? Heaven was his home
but mine the tomb in which he lay.

Here might I stay and sing
of him my soul adores;
never was love, dear King,
never was grief like yours! –
This is my friend in whose sweet praise
I all my days could gladly spend.

Samuel Crossman
Copyright © in this version Jubilate Hymns

98

NO SAFER PLACE TO BE
than in your will, O Lord;
no safer place to stand
than on your mighty word.

> *And this is my desire,*
> *this is the hunger of my heart:*
> *come, Holy Spirit fire,*
> *and set this child apart.*

No better place to be
than in your presence, Lord;
by faith we can draw near
through Christ, the living Word.

Geoff Baker
Copyright © 1994 Sovereign Music UK

98A

Sing to the Lord
from Psalm 96

Sing a new song to the Lord;

sing to the Lord, all the earth!

Sing to the Lord, praise his name;

proclaim his triumph day by day!

Worship the Lord in the splendour of
his holiness;

tremble before him all the earth!

For great is the Lord, and worthy to be
praised.

Amen.

© ℱ

99

O JESUS, I HAVE PROMISED
to serve you to the end –
be now and ever near me,
my Master and my Friend:
I shall not fear the battle
if you are by my side,
nor wander from the pathway
if you will be my guide.

O let me feel you near me –
the world is ever near;
I see the sights that dazzle,
the tempting sounds I hear;

my foes are ever near me,
around me and within:
but Jesus, draw still nearer
and shield my soul from sin!

O let me hear you speaking
in accents clear and still;
above the storms of passion,
the murmurs of self-will:
O speak to reassure me,
to hasten or control;
and speak to make me listen,
O Guardian of my soul.

O let me see your footmarks
and in them place my own:
my hope to follow truly
is in your strength alone.
O guide me, call me, draw me,
uphold me to the end;
and then in heaven receive me,
my Saviour and my Friend.

John Bode

100

O LET YOUR LOVE COME DOWN.

There is violence in the air,
fear touches all our lives.
How much pain can people bear?
Are we reaping what we've sown –
voices silent for too long?
We are calling:
'Let your love come down.'

There is power in your love,
bringing laughter out of tears:
it can heal the wounded soul.
In the streets where anger reigns
love will wash away the pain.
We are calling:
'Heaven's love, come down.'

Noel and Tricia Richards
Copyright © 1996 Kingsway's Thankyou Music

101

O RIGHTEOUS GOD

who searches minds and hearts,
bring to an end the violence of my foes
and make the righteous more secure,
O righteous God.

Sing praise to the name of the Lord most high,
sing praise to the name of the Lord most high;
give thanks to the Lord who rescues me,
O righteous God.

O Lord my God, I take refuge in you:
save and deliver me from all my foes –
my shield is God the Lord most high,
O Lord my God.

From Psalms 7,9,10,17
Maldwyn Pope
Copyright © 1989 Samsongs/Coronation Music Publishing/
Kingsway's Thankyou Music

102

OBEY THE MAKER'S INSTRUCTIONS

all the time!
Obey the maker's instructions
and you will find
obeying the maker's instructions
will help you see
that things fit together
much more easily!

Say you can buy a model of your favourite
classic car
without checking instructions you put it
together so far
but when you think you've finished you find a
little extra bit
it's the driver of the car, but now he just won't fit!

Say you read the Bible, to see what
God has said
and you find instructions and store them
in your head
but when you find you're tempted to doing
things the wrong way
instructions mean nothing unless you do
what they say!

Sammy Horner
© 1992 Daybreak Music

103

LEADER	**OH, THE LORD IS GOOD;**
ALL	oh, the Lord is good!
LEADER	The Lord is good;
ALL	the Lord is good!
LEADER	We want to hear you testify:
ALL	oh, the Lord is good.
LEADER	We want to hear you say:
ALL	the Lord is good.

continued over...

LEADER	We want to hear it loud and strong:
ALL	oh, the Lord is good.
LEADER	We want to hear you shout:
ALL	the Lord is good!

LEADER	We want to hear the children say:
CHILDREN	oh, the Lord is good.
LEADER	We want to hear you say:
CHILDREN	the Lord is good.
LEADER	We want to hear you loud and strong:
CHILDREN	oh, the Lord is good.
LEADER	We want to hear you shout:
CHILDREN	the Lord is good!

LEADER	We want to hear the brothers say:
MEN	oh, the Lord is good.
LEADER	We want to hear you say:
MEN	the Lord is good.
LEADER	We want to hear the sisters say:
WOMEN	oh, the Lord is good.
LEADER	We want to hear you say:
WOMEN	the Lord is good.

LEADER	The younger to the older say:
YOUNGER	oh, the Lord is good.
LEADER	We want to hear you say:
YOUNGER	the Lord is good.
LEADER	Older to the younger say:
OLDER	oh, the Lord is good.
LEADER	We want to hear you say:
OLDER	the Lord is good.

LEADER	Let every generation say:
ALL	oh, the Lord is good.
LEADER	We want to hear you say:
ALL	the Lord is good,
LEADER	so good,
ALL	so good;
LEADER	so kind,
ALL	so kind:
LEADER	give him glory,
ALL	give him glory
LEADER	all the time,
ALL	all the time.

Graham Kendrick
Copyright © 1996 Make Way Music

104

ONLY BY GRACE can we enter,
only by grace can we stand;
not by our human endeavour,
but by the blood of the Lamb.
Into your presence you call us,
you call us to come;
into your presence you draw us,
and now by your grace we come,
now by your grace we come.

Lord, if you mark our transgressions,
who will stand?
Thanks to your grace we are cleansed
by the blood of the Lamb.
Lord, if you mark …

Only by grace …

Gerrit Gustafson
Copyright © 1990 Integrity's Hosanna! Music
/Integrity Music Europe

105

OUR CONFIDENCE IS IN THE LORD,
the source of our salvation.
Rest is found in him alone,
the author of creation.
We will not fear the evil day
because we have a refuge;
in every circumstance we say,
'Our hope is built on Jesus.'
He is our fortress, we will never be shaken;
he is our fortress, we will never be shaken.
We will put our trust in God;
we will put our trust in God.

Noel & Tricia Richards
Copyright © 1989 Kingsway's Thankyou Music

106

OVER THE MOUNTAINS
AND THE SEA,
your river runs with love for me,
and I will open up my heart
and let the healer set me free.
I'm happy to be in the truth,
and I will daily lift my hands:
for I will always sing of when
your love came down. [Yeah!]

I could sing of your love for ever,
I could sing of your love for ever,
I could sing of your love for ever,
I could sing of your love for ever.

Over the mountains …

Oh, I feel like dancing –
it's foolishness I know;
but, when the world has seen the light,
they will dance with joy,
like we're dancing now.

Martin Smith
Copyright © 1994 Curious? Music UK/Kingsway's Thankyou Music

107

OVERWHELMED BY LOVE, deeper

than oceans,
high as the heavens;
ever-living God –
your love has rescued me.

All my sin was laid on your dear Son,
your precious one;
all my debt he paid –
great is your love for me.

No-one could ever earn your love;
your grace and mercy is free.
Lord, these words are true –
so is my love for you,
so is my love for you.

Noel Richards
Copyright © 1994 Kingsway's Thankyou Music

108

PEACE BE TO THESE STREETS,

peace be to these streets,
peace be to these streets
in the name of Jesus.

Peace be to these streets …

Walk here, Lord,
draw near, Lord:
pass through these streets today;
bring healing, forgiveness:
here let your living waters flow.

Love come to these streets,
love come to these streets,
love come to these streets
in the name of Jesus.

Joy come to these streets,
joy come to these streets,
joy come to these streets
in the name of Jesus.

… peace be to these streets.

Graham Kendrick
Copyright © 1996 Make Way Music

108A

For God's Blessing

O Lord, open our eyes to see what is
beautiful, our minds to know what is
true, and our hearts to love what is
good; for Jesus' sake. Amen.

© *From Prayers and Hymns for Junior Schools, reproduced*
by permission of Oxford University Press

109A

Sowing & Weeping

Eagerly I dug the ground
Then scattered the seed all around
The packet told me what to do
The sun was warm, the sky blue
Anticipation screamed at me
Fully grown plants I wanted to see
Out of the blue it began to rain
So I went back inside, again
Back to the daily grind
Pulling down the kitchen blind
With all those things to do, day after day
The sky's unremitting grey, I forgot to pray
After many days the sun came out
And I heard a sudden shout
"Darling, what are all these weeds?"
And what I saw brought me to my knees
Where I'd put a row of seeds
Grew something akin to trees
I pulled and cleared until
        my hands began to bleed
I fought and sought and began to plead
"Lord, what of the seed you've sown
What of the vision you've shown
Where is all the good you've done
What happened to what you've begun?
Why all these weeds?"
And God answered
"How else could I get you on your knees?"

© *Jonathan Cushrie, used by permission*

109

PRAISE GOD FROM WHOM ALL BLESSINGS FLOW,

praise him all creatures here below.
Praise him above you heavenly host,
praise Father, Son and Holy Ghost.

Give glory to the Father,
give glory to the Son,
give glory to the Spirit while endless ages run.
'Worthy the Lamb,' all heaven cries
to be exalted thus;
'Worthy the Lamb,' our hearts reply
for he was slain for us.

Praise God from whom all blessings flow,
praise God from whom all blessings flow.
Praise God …

After T. Ken
Andy Piercy & Dave Clifton
Copyright © 1993 IQ Music

110

PRAISE, MY SOUL, THE KING OF HEAVEN;

to his feet your tribute bring!
Ransomed, healed, restored, forgiven,
who like me his praise should sing?
      Alleluia, alleluia!
praise the everlasting King!

Praise him for his grace and favour
to our fathers in distress;
praise him still the same as ever,
slow to blame and swift to bless,
      Alleluia, alleluia!
glorious in his faithfulness!

Father-like, he tends and spares us;
all our hopes and fears he knows,
in his hands he gently bears us,
rescues us from all our foes,
      Alleluia, alleluia!
widely as his mercy flows.

Angels, help us to adore him –
you behold him face to face;
sun and moon, bow down before him –
praise him, all in time and space,
      Alleluia, alleluia!
praise with us the God of grace!

From Psalm 103
Henry Francis Lyte

111

PRAISE TO THE HOLIEST IN THE HEIGHT,

and in the depth be praise;
in all his words most wonderful,
most sure in all his ways!

Oh loving wisdom of our God!
when all was sin and shame,
a second Adam to the fight
and to the rescue came.

Oh wisest love! that flesh and blood,
which did in Adam fail,
should strive afresh against the foe,
should strive and should prevail.

And that the highest gift of grace
should flesh and blood refine:
God's presence and his very self,
and essence all-divine.

Oh generous love! that he who came
as man to smite our foe,
the double agony for us
as man should undergo.

And in the garden secretly,
and on the cross on high,
should teach his brethren, and inspire
to suffer and to die.

Praise to the Holiest in the height,
and in the depth be praise;
in all his words most wonderful,
most sure in all his ways!

John Newman

112

PURIFY MY HEART,

let me be as gold and precious silver;
purify my heart,
let me be as gold, pure gold.

Refiner's fire, my heart's one desire
is to be holy,
set apart for you, Lord;
I choose to be holy,
set apart for you, my Master,
ready to do your will.

Purify my heart,
cleanse me from within and make me holy;
purify my heart,
cleanse me from my sin, deep within.

Brian Doerkson
Copyright © 1990 Mercy/Vineyard Publishing/CopyCare

113

REACH OUT AND TAKE A HAND

and welcome one another;
reach out in Jesus' name –
let's welcome one another.
We come from many places,
but we belong together;
so many different faces,
but just one heavenly Father.

So let us sing together in harmony
and make the joyful sound of unity;
and as we worship Jesus,
we want the world to see his glory –
reach out and take a hand
and welcome one another.

Though we are many people,
yet we are one,
the sounds of many nations
join in one song;
rising from hearts that love him,
to fill the nations with his glory –
reach out and take a hand
and welcome one another.

Graham Kendrick
Copyright © 1996 Make Way Music

114

SALVATION BELONGS TO OUR GOD

who sits on the throne
and unto the Lamb:

Praise and glory, wisdom and thanks,
honour and power and strength
be to our God for ever and ever,
be to our God for ever and ever,
be to our God for ever and ever! Amen.

And we, the redeemed, shall be strong
in purpose and unity,
declaring aloud:

Adrian Howard & Pat Turner
Copyright © 1985 Restoration Music Ltd/Sovereign Music UK

115

SAVE THE PEOPLE, save the people now;

save the people, save the people now –
Lord have mercy.
Christ have mercy.
Father, hear our prayer:
save the people now.

Save the children, save the children now;
save the children, save the children now –
Lord have mercy.
Christ have mercy.
Father, hear our prayer:
save the children now.

Send your Spirit, send your Spirit now;
send your Spirit, send your Spirit now –
Lord have mercy.
Christ have mercy.
Father, hear our prayer:
send your Spirit now.

Send revival, send revival now;
send revival, send revival now –
Lord have mercy.
Christ have mercy.
Father, hear our prayer:
send revival now.

(Add verses as required)
Graham Kendrick
Copyright © 1996 Make Way Music

116

SEE, YOUR SAVIOUR COMES;

see, your Saviour comes.

Desolate cities, desolate homes,
desolate lives on the streets,
angry and restless,
when will you know
the things that would make
for your peace?

Father of mercy, hear as we cry
for all who live in this place;
show here your glory, come satisfy
your longing that all should be saved.

Where lives are broken,
let there be hope,
where there's division bring peace;
where there's oppression, judge and reprove
and rescue the crushed and the weak.

Lord, let your glory dwell in this land,
in mercy restore us again:
pour out salvation,
grant us your peace,
and strengthen the things that remain.

Graham Kendrick
Copyright © 1996 Make Way Music

117

SING TO THE LORD with all of your heart,
sing of the glory that's due to his name;
sing to the Lord with all of your soul,
join all of heaven and earth to proclaim:

You are the Lord, the Saviour of all,
God of creation, we praise you.
We sing the songs that awaken the dawn,
God of creation, we praise you.

Sing to the Lord with all of your mind,
with understanding give thanks to the King;
sing to the Lord with all of your strength,
living our lives as a praise offering.

Stuart Garrard
Copyright © 1994 Kingsway's Thankyou Music

117A

Confession

Almighty God, our heavenly Father, we
have sinned against you, through our
own fault, in thought and word and
deed, and in what we have left undone.
We are truly sorry and repent of all our
sins. For your Son our Lord Jesus
Christ's sake, forgive us all that is past,
and grant that we may serve you in
newness of life to the glory of your
name.

Amen.

© †

118

STAND UP, STAND UP FOR JESUS,

ye soldiers of the cross!
lift high his royal banner,
it must not suffer loss:
from victory unto victory
his army shall he lead
till every foe is vanquished
and Christ is Lord indeed.

Stand up, stand up for Jesus!
the trumpet call obey;
forth to the mighty conflict
in this his glorious day:
ye who are men, now serve him
against unnumbered foes;
let courage rise with danger,
and strength to strength oppose.

Stand up, stand up for Jesus!
stand in his strength alone,
the arm of flesh will fail you –
ye dare not trust your own:
put on the gospel armour,
each piece put on with prayer;
where duty calls, or danger,
be never wanting there.

Stand up, stand up for Jesus!
the strife will not be long;
this day the noise of battle,
the next the victor's song:
to him who overcometh,
a crown of life shall be;
he, with the King of glory,
shall reign eternally.

George Duffield Jr

119

STREAMS OF WORSHIP

and rivers of praise
ascending to the One who is the ancient of days:
to him who is worthy,
to him who was slain,
to him who sits upon the throne
and to the Lamb.

Thousands upon thousands encircle the throne
singing a new song to the One who is to come:
to him who is worthy,
to him who was slain,
to him who sits upon the throne
and to the Lamb:

'You are worthy, you are holy –
the Lord who was, the Lord who is,
The Lord who is to come;
you are mighty, you are awesome,
be praise and honour and glory for evermore.'

Streams of worship and rivers of praise
flowing from the lips of those
who never cease to be amazed
with him who is worthy,
with him who was slain,
with him who sits upon the throne
and with the Lamb:

From Revelation 4 & 5 David Hadden
Copyright © 1994 Restoration Music Ltd
/Sovereign Music UK

120

SUCH LOVE, pure as the whitest snow,
such love, weeps for the shame I know,
such love, paying the debt I owe –
O Jesus, such love!

Such love, stilling my restlessness,
such love, filling my emptiness,
such love, showing me holiness –
O Jesus, such love!

Such love springs from eternity,
such love, streaming through history,
such love, fountain of life to me –
O Jesus, such love!

Graham Kendrick
Copyright © 1988 Make Way Music

121

SURELY OUR GOD *is the God of gods*
and the Lord of kings,
a revealer of mysteries.
Surely our God …

He changes the times and the seasons,
he gives rhythm to the tides;
he knows what is hidden
in the darkest of places,
brings the shadows into his light.

I will praise you always, my Father –
you are Lord of heaven and earth,
you hide your secrets
from the wise and the learned
and reveal them to this your child.

Thank you for sending your only Son,
we may know the mystery of God –
he opens the treasures
of wisdom and knowledge
to the humble, not to the proud.

David and Liz Morris
Copyright © 1996 Tevita Music

122

TAKE MY LIFE and let it be
consecrated, Lord, to thee;
take my hands and let them move
at the impulse of thy love,
at the impulse of thy love.

Take my feet and let them be
swift and beautiful for thee;
take my voice and let me sing
always, only, for my King,
always, only, for my King.

Take my silver and my gold –
not a mite would I withhold;
take my moments and my days,
let them flow in ceaseless praise,
let them flow in ceaseless praise.

Take my will and make it thine,
it shall be no longer mine;
take my heart, it is thine own –
it shall be thy royal throne,
it shall be thy royal throne.

Frances R.Havergal

122A

Matthew 24:36, 37, 40–42

No-one knows about that day or hour,
not even the angels in heaven, not the
Son, but only the Father. As it was in
the days of Noah, so it will be at the
coming of the Son of Man. Two men
will be in a field; one will be taken and
the other left. Two women will be
grinding with a hand mill; one will be
taken and the other left. Therefore,
keep watch, because you do not know
what day your Lord will come.

123

THANK YOU FOR SAVING ME

– what can I say?
You are my everything, I will sing your praise.
You shed your blood for me – what can I say?
You took my sin and shame,
a sinner called by name.

Great is the Lord,
great is the Lord!
For we know your truth has set us free,
you've set your hope in me.

Mercy and grace are mine, forgiven is my sin –
Jesus my only hope, the Saviour of the world.
'Great is the Lord,' we cry,
'God, let your kingdom come!'
Your word has let me see,
thank you for saving me.

… Thank you for saving me – what can I say?

Martin J.Smith
Copyright © 1993 Curious? Music UK/Kingsway's Thankyou Music

124

THE CRUCIBLE FOR SILVER,

and the furnace for gold,
but the Lord tests the heart of this child.
Standing in all purity,
God, our passion is for holiness:
lead us to the secret place of praise.

Jesus, holy One,
you are my heart's desire;
King of kings, my everything,
you've set this heart on fire.
Jesus, holy One …

Father, take our offering,
with our song we humbly praise you;
you have brought your holy fire to our lips.
Standing in your beauty, Lord,
your gift to us is holiness:
lead us to the place where we can sing:

Martin J.Smith
Copyright © 1993 Kingsway's Thankyou Music

125

THE GOD OF ABRAHAM PRAISE

who reigns enthroned above;
the ancient of eternal days
and God of love!
The Lord, the great I AM,
by earth and heaven confessed –
we bow before his holy name
for ever blessed.

To him we lift our voice
at whose supreme command
from death we rise to gain the joys
at his right hand:
we all on earth forsake –
it's wisdom, fame and power;
the God of Israel we shall make
our shield and tower.

Though nature's strength decay,
and earth and hell withstand,
at his command we fight our way
to Canaan's land:
the water's deep we pass
with Jesus in our view,
and through the howling wilderness
our path pursue.

He by his name has sworn –
on this we shall depend,
and as on eagles' wings upborne
to heaven ascend:
there we shall see his face,
his power we shall adore,
and sing the wonders of his grace
for evermore.

There rules the Lord our king,
the Lord our righteousness,
victorious over death and sin,
the Prince of Peace:
on Zion's sacred height
his kingdom he maintains,
and glorious with his saints in light
for ever reigns.

Triumphant hosts on high
give thanks eternally
and 'Holy, holy, holy' cry,
'great Trinity!'
Hail Abraham's God and ours!
one mighty hymn we raise,
all power and majesty be yours
and endless praise!

From a Hebrew Doxology transcribed by M.Lyon Adapted by
T.Olivers Copyright © in this version Jubilee Hymns

126

THERE IS A LOUDER SHOUT TO COME,

there is a sweeter song to hear;
all the nations with one voice,
all the people with one fear.
Bowing down before your throne,
every tribe and tongue we'll be;
all the nations with one voice,
all the people with one king.
And what a song we'll sing upon that day.

O what a song we'll sing, and
O what a tune we'll bear –
you deserve an anthem
    of the highest praise;
O what a joy will rise, and
O what a sound we'll make –
you deserve an anthem
    of the highest praise.

Now we see a part of this,
one day we shall see in full;
all the nations with one voice,
all the people with one love.
No one else will share your praise,
nothing else can take your place;
all the nations with one voice,
all the people with one Lord.
And what a song we'll sing upon that day.

Even now upon the earth,
there's a glimpse of all to come;
many people with one voice,
harmony of many tongues.
We will all confess your name,
you will be our only praise;
all the nations with one voice,
all the people with one God.
And what a song we'll sing upon that day ...

Matt Redman
Copyright © 1996 Kingsway's Thankyou Music

126A

The Creed

Let us affirm our faith in God:
We believe and trust in God the Father who made the world.
We believe and trust in his Son Jesus Christ, who redeemed mankind.
We believe and trust in his Holy Spirit, who gives life to the people of God.
We believe and trust in one God: Father, Son and Holy Spirit.
Amen.

© ℣

126B

The Lord's Prayer
from Matthew 6 and Luke 11

Our Father in heaven, hallowed be your name, your kingdom come, your will be done, on earth as it is in heaven. Give us today our daily bread. Forgive us our sins as we forgive those who sin against us. Lead us not into temptation but deliver us from evil. For the kingdom, the power and the glory are yours, now and for ever.
Amen.

127

THERE IS NO ONE LIKE OUR GOD
in all the earth,
there is no one like our God in all the earth,
no one like our God, no one like our God.

Our God has made the heavens,
our God has made the earth;
and everything that lives
his word has brought to birth.

He numbers every star
and calls each one by name;
he fills the skies with clouds,
supplies the earth with rain.

Sing praises unto God,
sing praises to his name;
his love will never end,
his word will never fail.

... God is with us;
God is with us;
God is with us.

Noel and Tricia Richards
Copyright © 1996 Kingsway's Thankyou Music

128

THERE IS A REDEEMER,
Jesus, God's own Son,
precious Lamb of God, Messiah,
Holy One.

Thank you, O my Father,
for giving us your Son,
and leaving your Spirit
til the work on earth is done.

Jesus, my Redeemer,
name above all names,
precious Son of God, Messiah,
Lamb for sinners slain:

When I stand in glory
I will see his face,
and there I'll serve my King for ever
in that holy place.

Melody Green
Copyright © 1982 Birdwing Music/Ears to Hear Music
/BMG Songs Inc/Alliance Media Ltd/CopyCare Ltd

128A

Responses
from Matthew 5:3

Blessed are the poor in spirit:

for theirs is the kingdom of heaven.

Blessed are those who hunger and thirst
for righteousness:

for they will be filled.

Praise the Lord:

The Lord's name be praised!

Amen.

© ✢

129

THERE IS POWER IN THE NAME OF JESUS –
we believe in his name.
We have called on the name of Jesus:
we are saved, we are saved!
At his name the demons flee,
at his name captives are freed;
for there is no other name
that is higher than Jesus.

There is power in the name of Jesus,
like a sword in our hands.
We declare in the name of Jesus:
we shall stand, we shall stand!
At his name, God's enemies
shall be crushed beneath our feet;
for there is no other name
that is higher than Jesus.

Noel Richards
Copyright © 1989 Kingsway's Thankyou Music

129A

Prayer For Forgiveness From The Past And Strength For The Future

Almighty God, my gracious Heavenly Father, I have sinned against you. In your great mercy, come to me in the fire of your love. Please grant me your forgiveness, wash me clean, hide my past behind your back, fill me with your Holy Spirit and set my feet firmly in your way. I ask these things in the name and for the sake of your lovely Son Jesus.

Amen.

130A

Prayer for Courage

Our Heavenly Father, your Son left his glory for the sorrow of mankind: grant us the strength to leave behind our comfort and security, to take up the cross of our Saviour and follow where he leads; for his name's sake.

Amen.

© *Michael Perry* ✢

130

THERE'S NO VEIL ANY LONGER

to separate the church
from the presence of the Lord;
there's no veil any longer:
we enter with sincere and grateful hearts.

Lord, we come into your courts
with a sacrifice of praise;
Lord, we come in confidence
with a sacrifice of praise.
Creator of all heaven and earth,
we are wonderfully made;
Lord of all the universe,
we are gloriously saved:
boldly we approach the throne,
we are yours and not our own –
for who you are,
for what you've done,
we worship you.

… There's no veil, there's no veil.

David Hadden
Copyright © 1996 Restoration Music Ltd.

131

THESE ARE THE DAYS OF ELIJAH,

declaring the word of the Lord;
and these are the days of your servant, Moses,
righteousness being restored.
And though these are days of great trial,
of famine and darkness and sword,
still we are the voice in the desert crying,
'Prepare ye the way of the Lord.'

Behold he comes riding on the clouds,
shining like the sun at the trumpet call;
lift your voice it's the year of jubilee,
out of Zion's hill salvation comes.

These are the days of Ezekiel,
the dry bones becoming as flesh;
and these are the days of your servant, David,
rebuilding a temple of praise.
These are the days of the harvest,
the fields are as white in the world,
and we are the labourers in your vineyard
declaring the word of the Lord:

Robin Mark
Copyright © 1996 Daybreak Music

132

THEY THAT WAIT ON THE LORD

will renew their strength,
run and not grow weary,
walk and not faint.

Do you not know? Have you not heard?
My Father does not grow weary,
he'll give passion to a willing heart;
even the youths get tired and faint,
but strength will come for those who wait.

… I will wait, I will wait, I will wait on you;
I will run, I will run, I will run with you;
my love, my love, my love for you.

From Isaiah 40
Kevin Prosch
Copyright © 1995 7th Time Music/Kingsway's Thankyou Music

133

THINE BE THE GLORY, risen,

conquering Son,
endless is the victory thou o'er death hast won.
Angels in bright raiment rolled the stone away,
kept the folded grave-clothes where thy body lay.

Thine be the glory,
risen, conquering Son,
endless is the victory
thou o'er death hast won!

Lo, Jesus meets us, risen from the tomb!
Lovingly he greet us, scatters fear and gloom.
Let the Church with gladness hymns of
triumph sing,
for her Lord now liveth, death has lost its sting.

No more we doubt thee, glorious Prince of Life;
life is nought without thee: aid us in our strife;
make us more than conquerors,
through thy deathless love;
bring us safe through Jordan to thy home above.

E.L. Budry
Tr. R.B. Hoyle

43

132A

For strength to follow Jesus

from Matthew 5

Jesus said: 'If one of you wants to be great, he must be the servant of the rest.' – Master, we hear your call,
help us to follow.

Jesus said: 'Unless you change and become humble like little children, you can never enter the kingdom of heaven.' – Master, we hear your call,
help us to follow.

Jesus said: 'Happy are those who are humble; they will receive what God has promised.' – Master we hear your call, help us to follow.
Jesus said: 'Be merciful just as your Father is merciful; love your enemies and do good to them.' – Master, we hear your call,
help us to follow.

Jesus said: 'Love one another, just as I have loved you; the greatest love a person can have for his friends is to give his life for them.' – Master, we hear your call,
help us to follow.

Jesus said: 'Go to all peoples everywhere and make them my disciples, and I will be with you always, to the end of the world.' – Master, we hear your call,
help us to follow.

Lord, you have redeemed us and called us to your service: give us grace to hear your word and to obey your commandment; for your mercy's sake.

Amen.

134

THOUGH I FEEL AFRAID

of territory unknown,
I know that I can say
that I do not stand alone
for, Jesus, you have promised
your presence in my heart –
I cannot see the ending,
but it's here that I must start.

And all I know is you have called me
and that I will follow is all I can say;
I will go where you will send me
and your fire lights the way.

What lies across the waves
may cause my heart to fear –
will I survive the day,
must I leave what's known and dear?
A ship that's in the harbour
is still and safe from harm,
but it was not built to be there:
it was made for wind and storm.

Ian White

135

TO BE IN YOUR PRESENCE,

to sit at your feet,
where your love surrounds me,
and makes me complete:

This is my desire, O Lord,
this is my desire;
this is my desire, O Lord,
this is my desire.

To rest in your presence,
not rushing away,
to cherish each moment –
here I would stay:

Noel Richards

135A

Proverbs 2:1, 2, 5–8

If you accept my words and store up my commands within you, turning your ear to wisdom and applying your heart to understanding, then you will understand the fear of the Lord and find the knowledge of God. For the Lord gives wisdom, and from his mouth come knowledge and understanding. He holds victory in store for the upright, he is a shield to those whose walk is blameless, for he guards the course of the just and protects the way of his faithful ones.

136

TO SEE WITH YOUR EYES

beyond these four walls,
the plight of the helpless
beyond the shadow that falls;
to pull back the curtain on all you survey,
the lost and the broken
who cry to find a new day.
Send a vision through the twilight,
changing us that we might

See with your eyes –
healing our blindness,
removing the scales,
let us see with your eyes;
throw back the shutters
and give us new sight, Lord,
that we might see a dying world
with your eyes.

To see with your eyes,
to feel with your heart,
give us compassion,
our souls awake from the dark;
empower your people to rise to the call,
heeding your heart's cry
that we might serve with our all.
Send a vision through the twilight,
changing us that we might

Johnny Markin
Copyright © 1996 Daybreak Music

137

TURN OUR HEARTS, turn our hearts.

Turn our hearts to one another,
let your kindness show:
where our words or deeds have wounded,
let forgiveness flow.

Turn our hearts from pride and anger
to your ways of peace,
for you died and shed your blood
that enmity may cease.

Turn the hearts of generations
that we may be one:
make us partners in the kingdom
til your work is done.

As we all have been forgiven,
so must we forgive;
as we all have found acceptance,
so let us receive.

… Turn our hearts,
change our hearts,
join our hearts,
turn our hearts.

Graham Kendrick
Copyright © 1996 Make Way Music

137A

The Eucharistic Prayer

The Lord is here.
His Spirit is with us.

Lift up your hearts.
We lift them to the Lord.

Let us give thanks to the Lord our God.
It is right to give him thanks and praise.

© ASB 1980.

138

WE SEE JESUS –

for his suffering crowned with glory and
    with praise,
tasting death for all men by God's grace,
given power to put all things in place;
and we see Jesus –
seated at the right hand of the throne,
making intercession for his own,
upholding all things by his word alone.

For you are glorious! shining victorious
over powers and principalities;
for you are glorious! shining victorious,
disarming all your enemies:
the rulers of this world beneath your
    feet are hurled
as you reign, our conquering King.

David W.Morris & Mike Massa

We praise you, Lord God, that nothing yet seen
can compare with the glory to come;
we praise you, Lord God, that what has been
    revealed
is a foretaste of heaven begun:
never excluded from your love,
living as children and free;
you have prepared a place for us,
a home for eternity;
you have prepared a place for us,
a home for eternity.

Jesus,
our Lord,
author of life,
friend for eternity.

Phil Lawson-Johnston
Copyright © 1996 Cloud Music/Soveriegn Music UK

139

WE PRAISE YOU, LORD GOD,

    you've made yourself known
to those who believe in your name;
we praise you, Lord God, your love has been shown.
You've carried our sin and our shame,
you have declared to those who believe,
where you are we now can be
for you have prepared a place for us,
a home for eternity;
for you have prepared a place for us,
a home for eternity.

We praise you, Lord God, you have proclaimed
your dwelling place will be with man;
we praise you, Lord God, for ever the same.
You determined before time began
that those who believe and call on your name
shall open their eyes and see
that you have prepared a place for us
where death has no victory;
that you have prepared a place for us
where death has no victory.

There will be no more suffering,
there'll be no more pain;
you will wipe every tear from our eyes.
There will be no more sorrow,
there'll be no more death –
just glorious fullness of life.

140

WE WANT TO CHANGE THIS WORLD,

we want to change this world;
we want to change this world,
we want to change this world.

So wave those flags of justice over the nations
and hit those drums of peace among the peoples,
we hear the sound of history in the making –
let God's love run around the earth and
    bring freedom!

So hold each other's hands across the oceans
and play those chords of peace among the peoples,
we hear the sound of reconciliation –
let God's love dance around the earth and
    bring freedom!

… And we want to change this world
as we live out holy lives;
and we want to change this world
as you wash our motives clean.
And we want to change this world
as we live out holy lives;
and we want to change this world
as you wash our motives clean –
oh, wash us clean!

Sue Rinaldi
Copyright © 1996 Kingway's Thankyou Music

141

WE WANT TO SEE JESUS LIFTED HIGH –

a banner that flies across this land;
that all men might see the truth and know
he is the way to heaven.
We want to see Jesus lifted high –
a banner that flies across this land;
that all men might see the truth and know
he is the way to heaven.

We want to see, we want to see,
we want to see Jesus lifted high.
We want to see, we want to see,
we want to see Jesus lifted high.

Step by step we're moving forward,
little by little taking ground;
every prayer a powerful weapon:
strongholds come tumbling down,
and down,
and down,
and down.

We want to see Jesus lifted high ...

We're gonna see, we're gonna see,
we're gonna see Jesus lifted high.
We're gonna see, we're gonna see,
we're gonna see Jesus lifted high.

Doug Horley
Copyright © 1993 Kingsway's Thankyou Music

142

WE WORSHIP AND ADORE YOU, LORD –

hear us when we call,
for there is no god above you,
you are the Lord of all.

But how can we begin to express
what's on our hearts?
There are no words enough, Lord,
for us to even start.

The tongues of men and angels
we need, to sing your praise,
so that we may glorify your name
through heaven's eternal days.

There was no other good enough
to pay the price of sin,
you, only, could unlock
the gate of heaven and let us in.

So, we worship and adore you ...

Andy Piercy
v.3 words: Cecil F. Alexander (Traditional) © 1995 IQ Music

143

WE'RE HERE FOR THE HARVEST,

get ready to reap,
the call is for action, it's not time to sleep;
we're here for the harvest, the yield will be great,
the fields are now ripened so don't hesitate.

There's need for more labourers –
for many not few –
the challenge set before us is: who?
And we cry, 'Lord of the harvest,
in this day of your power,
hear the anthem of voices – send me!
Send me, send me,
Lord of the harvest, send me!
Send me, send me,
Lord of the harvest, send me.'

The Spirit is upon us to cause the blind to see,
the Spirit of the Sovereign Lord to
set the captive free;
the homeless and the needy can
no longer be ignored,
and all oppressed will celebrate
the favour of the Lord.

Chris Bowater
Copyright © 1996 Sovereign Lifestyle Music

144

WELCOME THE KING,

welcome the King,
welcome the King
who comes in the name of the Lord.

Who is this King,
who is this King,
who is this King,
who is this King,
who is this King
who comes in the name of the Lord?

Clear the road before him,
open the ancient doors,
let every heart receive him:
welcome the King
who comes in the name of the Lord.

He is the King of glory,
crucified and risen;
he is the Lord Almighty:
welcome the King
who comes in the name of the Lord;
welcome the King
who comes in the name of the Lord.

Graham Kendrick
Copyright © 1996 Make Way Music

144A

2 Corinthians 5: 17

If anyone is in Christ, he is a new creation; the old has gone, the new has come!

145

WELL, I HEAR THEY'RE SINGING

in the streets that Jesus is alive,
and all creation shouts aloud that Jesus is alive;
now surely we can all be changed
'cause Jesus is alive;
and everybody here can know that Jesus is alive.

And I will live for all my days
to raise a banner of truth and light,
to sing about my Saviour's love
and the best thing that happened –
it was the day I met you.

I've found Jesus,
I've found Jesus,
I've found Jesus,
I've found Jesus.

Well, I feel like dancing in the streets
'cause Jesus is alive,
to join with all who celebrate that Jesus is alive.
The joy of God is in this town
'cause Jesus is alive;
for everybody's seen the truth that Jesus is alive.

And I will live for all my days
to raise a banner of truth and light,
to sing about my Saviour's love
and the best thing that happened –
it was the day I met you.

Well, you lifted me from where I was,
set my feet upon a rock –
humbled that you even know about me.
Now I have chosen to believe,
believing that you've chosen me;
I was lost but now I've found –

Martin Smith
Copyright © 1994 Curious? Music UK/Kingsway's Thankyou Music

146

WHAT A FRIEND I'VE FOUND,

closer than a brother;
I have felt your touch,
more intimate than lovers.

Jesus, Jesus, Jesus,
friend for ever.

What a hope I've found,
more faithful than a mother;
it would break my heart
to ever lose each other.

Martin Smith
Copyright © 1996 Curious? Music UK/Kingsway's Thankyou Music

147

WHEN I LOOK TO THE HEAVENS

created by your hands,
I see the moon and the stars
that your fingers set in place;
yet you care for me
with a love so deep –
O Lord, you are so great!

Children sing to your name
to silence all your foes;
O Lord, your name is so powerful,

147A

A Covenant Service

As a company of men and women
who have received Christ as Saviour
and by grace become God's children,
we here and now dedicate ourselves
to him; we desire to renew our
commitment as a church of Jesus
Christ, indwelt by the Holy Spirit,
united to walk worthily of our
profession, set apart to proclaim his
word, to observe his commandments,
and by God's grace to work according
to his will for the salvation of others
and the well-being of his world.

Amen.

© A Covenant Service ☙

too wonderful for words,
yet you care for me
with a love so deep –
O Lord, you are so great!

From the earth and sky
to the deep of the sea,
Lord, you care so much for me.
From the earth …

When I look …

148

WHEN I SURVEY the wondrous cross
on which the Prince of Glory died,
my richest gain I count as loss,
and pour contempt on all my pride.

Forbid it, Lord, that I should boast
save in the cross of Christ my God:
the very things that charm me most –
I sacrifice them to his blood.

See from his head, his hands, his feet,
sorrow and love flow mingled down:
when did such love and sorrow meet
or thorns compose so rich a crown?

Were the whole realm of nature mine,
that were an offering far too small;
love so amazing, so divine,
demands my soul, my life, my all!

Isaac Watts

149

WHEN THERE'S HARD TIMES or
   there's good times,
when the rain falls or the sun shines,
when you test me or you bless me
my resolve will none the less be:

I will love you come what may,
I will love you every day;
I will love you now and for evermore.

When there's dark clouds or there's clear skies,
when it's sunset or it's sunrise,
when I'm needy or I've plenty,
Lord, not one thing will prevent me:

When your presence seems so distant,
when my doubts seem so persistent,

then no matter how I'm feeling,
Lord, in one thing I'm unyielding:

When the battle seems so endless,
when I'm feeling so defenceless,
when the enemy surrounds me
and his arrows fly around me:

When my future is uncertain,
when my heart is heavy-burdened,
when I'm tired or I'm hurting,
Lord, in one thing I'm determined:

When the past seems to pursue me,
when temptation whispers to me,
when my worst fears are awakened,
Lord, on one thing I'm unshaken:

150

WHEN WE'RE IN TROUBLE, when
   there are cares,
when faith is shaken up, when we despair,
we call on Jesus, give him our thanks,
we let his peace and joy come to our hearts.

We're going to keep on praying,
keep on praying;
we're going to keep on praying,
keep on praying.

When there is sickness, when there is pain,
there is a healing touch each time we pray;
God always listens, cares for our needs,
prayers of the righteous ones have power indeed.

We're going to keep on …

Prayers for the nation, prayers for the world,
prayers for the government,
   prayers for the church;
prayers for the seekers, prayers for the saints,
praying that people will come to faith.

151

WHERE IS THE WISE MAN who fears
   the Lord,
who walks in all his ways,
following God with all his heart
and serving all his days?
For the fear of the Lord teaches wisdom,
the fear of the Lord leads to life;
the Spirit of the Lord will rest upon him
who makes the fear of the Lord his delight.

continued over…

Let the fear of the Lord be upon us,
let godly fear be before our eyes;
let the fear of the Lord be our wisdom,
let godly fear be to us the light of life.

The Lord God has shown us what is good
and what he requires of us:
to act justly and to love mercy,
to walk humbly with our God.
The fear of the Lord is a refuge,
a fortress in which we can hide;
his mercy extends to those who fear him,
they are those in whom he confides.

So who from among us will fear the Lord
and obey his every word,
no longer walk blindly in darkness
but trust in the name of God?
For to fear his name is wisdom,
to fear his name is life –
O Spirit of God, rest upon us
as we make the fear of God our delight.

Phil Lawson-Johnston
© 1996 Cloud Music/Sovereign UK Music

151A

Prayer For Peace
In The World

Almighty Father, whose will is to restore all
things in your beloved Son, the King of all:
govern the hearts and minds of those in
authority, and bring the families of the
nations, divided and torn apart by the
ravages of sin, to be subject to his just and
gentle rule; who is alive and reigns with
you and the Holy Spirit, one God, now and
for ever.

Amen.

© Pentecost 15 Collect ASB 1980

152

WHERE TWO OR THREE of you gather
in my name,
I am there, I am there with you;
and if just two of you stand in agreement
as you pray gathered in my name,

my Father will hear your prayer,
hear your prayer and answer
and will give you anything you ask
in my name.

From Matthew 18
Graham Kendrick
Copyright © 1996 Make Way Music

153

WHO HAS LAID THE
EARTH'S FOUNDATIONS,

measured out its length and breadth
when the morning stars all sang together
and all the sons of God shouted for joy?

Who has sealed the ocean's boundaries,
so contained its raging power?
When the word went forth from heaven's glory,
the fountains of the deep were held at bay!

He's the Lord of hosts,
he's the King of glory;
lift up on high the name of the Lord!
He's the Lord of creation,
God of our salvation;
lift up on high the name of the Lord!

Who commands the light of morning,
caused the dawn to know its place,
as the darkness flees his holy presence
and evil men take flight from his glorious grace?

From Job 38
Johnny Markin
Copyright © 1996 Daybreak Music

154

WHO WILL CALL HIM
KING OF KINGS,

who will call him Lord of lords,
who will call him Prince of Peace,
such a wonderful counsellor, mighty God.

We will call him King of kings
we will call him Lord of lords,
we will call him Prince of Peace,
such a wonderful counsellor, mighty God.

I will call him King of kings
I will call him Lord of lords,
I will call him Prince of Peace,
such a wonderful counsellor, mighty God.

Greg Nelson, Bob Farrell and Sandi Patti-Helvering
Copyright © 1990 Sandi's Songs Music/Word Music Inc/Dayspring
Music/Summerdawn Music/Gentle Ben Music/CopyCare

154A

John 14:6

Jesus said, 'I am the way, the truth and the life. No one comes to the Father except through me.'

You are righteous
and your perfect truth shall reign –
nothing can escape your holy gaze.

Without beginning or end
is the love of God for those he has created.
There will come a day
when all the tears and sorrow have to end:
for ever we will live and reign with him,
our mighty King who holds eternity.

Leon Evans, Jon & Linsey Grant
Copyright © 1996 Church Music

155

WHOLEHEARTED, wholehearted
in my praise to you,
in my praise to you.

Completely, completely
I worship you,
Lord, I worship you.

Abandoned in my love
and focused in my gaze,
my heart is overflowing
with thankfulness and praise.

A sense of purifying
and cleansing by your grace –
wholeheartedly,
wholeheartedly I praise.
A sense of purifying …

Trish Morgan
Copyright © 1995 Sovereign Lifestyle Music

156A

Praise Him All You Nations
from Psalm 117

Praise the Lord, all you nations;
extol him all you peoples.

For his love protecting us is strong;
his faithfulness endures for ever.

Amen

© ✝

156

WITHOUT BEGINNING OR END,
before the earth was formed
and the mountains were created,
you have reigned.
Through all the generations, you are Lord;
a thousand years are but as yesterday to you,
lives are gone as quickly as a dream.

Still you notice me –
you who rule the nations –
and you died for me as great as you are;
you've let me see your power
and your mercy:
I am humbled, Lord, I am yours,
I am yours.

How great you are,
robed with honour and with majesty and light;
the heavens are your throne,
you created light and darkness, sea and sky.

157

YOU ARE LORD OF OUR HEARTS;
you are Lord of our lives
and you reign,
and you reign.
You are Lord …

His wave of love will wash away
our prejudice and shame,
our brokenness and pain;
then faith will rise,
faith instead of fear –
connected in his love,
anointed from above.

You are Lord of my soul,
you are Lord – come, take control;
and you reign,
and you reign in my heart.

Trish Morgan
Copyright © 1996 Radical UK Music/Sovereign Music UK

158

YOU ARE THE SOURCE of my inspiration.
You broke the wall of alienation
becoming flesh and blood,
sharing our humanity,
identifying with us,
choosing vulnerability,
moving into the neighbourhood:
thank You for entering into our world,
thank You for entering into our world,
thank You for entering into our world,
thank You for entering into our world.

Jon Baker
Copyright © 1996 Serious Music UK

159

YOU LAID ASIDE YOUR MAJESTY,

gave up everything for me,
suffered at the hands of those you had created;
you took all my guilt and shame,
when you died and rose again –
now today you reign in heaven and earth exalted.

I really want to worship you, my Lord;
you have won my heart and I am yours
for ever and ever:
I will love you.

You are the only one who died for me,
gave your life to set me free,
so I lift my voice to you
in adoration.

Noel Richards
Copyright © 1985 Kingsway's Thankyou Music

160

YOU'RE THE LION OF JUDAH,

the Lamb that was slain,
you ascended to heaven and evermore will reign;
at the end of the age when the earth you reclaim,
you will gather the nations before you.

And the eyes of all men will be fixed
on the Lamb who was crucified,
for with wisdom and mercy and justice
he reigns at the Father's side.

And the angels will cry: 'Hail the Lamb
who was slain for the world – rule in power.'
And the earth will reply: 'You shall reign
as the King of all kings and
the Lord of all lords.'

There's a shield in our hand and
a sword at our side,
there's a fire in our spirit that cannot be denied;
as the Father has told us: for these you have died,
for the nations that gather before you.

And the ears of all men need to hear
of the Lamb who was crucified,
who descended to hell yet was raised up
to reign at the Father's side.

Robin Mark
Copyright © 1996 Daybreak Music Ltd.

Index

Song titles differing from first lines are in italics

Index of Prayers & Liturgy